LAWS OF HIDDEN ABUNDANCE
and the Path to Wealth

Apply Universal Principles to
Create Lasting Prosperity and
Purpose

Copyright © 2025 Lucian Rae
All rights reserved.

ISBN: 979-8-89965-069-7

No part of this publication may be reproduced, stored in a retrieval system, or transmitted in any form or by any means—electronic, mechanical, photocopying, recording, or otherwise—without the prior written permission of the author or publisher. All rights reserved under international and Pan-American copyright conventions.

Legal Notice: This publication is intended for personal use only. You may not modify, distribute, sell, use, quote, or paraphrase any part of this book without explicit consent from the author or publisher.

Disclaimer: The information contained within this book is provided for educational and entertainment purposes only. The author and publisher have made every effort to ensure the accuracy and completeness of the information presented. However, no warranties of any kind are expressed or implied. This book does not constitute legal, financial, medical, or professional advice. Readers should consult qualified professionals before applying any of the information contained herein. By reading this book, the reader agrees that the author and publisher shall not be held liable for any damages, losses, or liabilities caused directly or indirectly by the use or misuse of the information contained in this book, including but not limited to errors, omissions, or inaccuracies.

This book was written with love and intention by someone who walked the path from fear to faith, from scarcity to hidden abundance.

Table of Contents

Introduction 5

The Law of Divine Inheritance 12
The Law of Belief and Perception 24
The Law of Worthiness 35
The Law of Alignment 45
The Law of Divine Timing 55
The Law of Embodiment 65
The Law of Inspired Action 75
The Law of Receiving 87
The Law of Circulation 96
The Law of Expansion 106
The Law of Devotion 116
The Law Beyond the Law 126

Wealth in Motion: How the 12 Laws Turn Abundance into Financial Reality 136
   How the 12 Laws Shape Your Financial Life 138
   PART ONE: You Want to Start Something New 142
   PART TWO: You Want to Rise Where You Already Are .. 160

Introduction

The True Meaning of Wealth

You were never meant to chase wealth.
You were meant to remember it.

Not just the kind that fills bank accounts or buys time —
but the wealth that lives in your breath,
your being,
your belonging to something sacred and infinite.

True wealth is not earned.
It is remembered.
It is received.
It is revealed.

We live in a world obsessed with achieving, accumulating, and proving —
but the deepest abundance can't be grasped through striving.

It is found in **alignment**.
It flows through **surrender**.
It speaks in **stillness**.

And here is the truth most people miss:
When you remember who you are,
when you align with the source of all creation,
financial abundance is not excluded — it becomes inevitable.

This book is not about choosing between money and meaning.
It is about unlocking both.
It is about **embodying a wealth that is spiritual in origin, and physical in expression.**
Peace *and* provision.

Faith *and* overflow.
Stillness *and* success.

This book is a journey back to the truth:
You are already enough.
You are already abundant.
And now — it's time to receive what has always been yours.

What Is Hidden Abundance?

Abundance is not far away.
It is not locked in the future, waiting for you to become better, richer, or more deserving.

Abundance is here — now.
But it is hidden.
Not because it is missing…
but because **we've been taught not to see it.**

We've inherited a world of forgetfulness.
We've been taught to measure wealth by numbers, not by truth.
To look outward before looking inward.
To strive instead of surrender.
To believe that scarcity is more realistic than joy.

But hidden abundance is real.
It is the current beneath your fear.
The quiet "yes" beneath your doubt.
The divine provision that has always been assigned to you — waiting to be received.

Hidden abundance is **not just a feeling** — though it may start there.
It is a *reality* you begin to unlock when you align with the spiritual laws that govern creation.

It includes:

- Peace in your nervous system
- Confidence in your choices
- Money that flows without guilt
- Opportunities that meet you where you are

- A life that reflects your inner truth

This is not about pretending you're abundant while secretly feeling broken or behind.

This is about *remembering the truth so deeply that the world begins to rearrange around it.*

When you shift from fear to faith…
When you stop asking "How will it happen?" and start saying "Yes"…
When you walk with vision instead of worry…

The hidden becomes visible.
What you once chased… starts to find you.
Not because you've forced it, but because you've become a match for it.

This is hidden abundance:
The kind of wealth that rises from within and then takes shape without.
The kind that honors both spirit and form.
The kind that doesn't ask you to choose between money and meaning — but leads you to both.

It's been waiting.
Now, it's your turn to remember.

Why This Path Is Different

You've probably heard that you need to hustle harder.
Visualize more.
Raise your vibration.
Fix your mindset.
Work until you deserve it.

Maybe you've even whispered to yourself:
"Why does it feel like abundance works for everyone but me?"

You are not broken.
You are not blocked.
You are not behind.

You've simply been walking a path that was built on fear, force, and fragments.
A path that told you:

- You must prove your worth
- Receiving is selfish
- Struggle is spiritual
- Money and meaning are opposites

But this path — the one you're on now — is different.

This is the path of **alignment over effort.**
Trust over control.
Faith over fear.
Truth over performance.

This is not about faking positivity or forcing success.
It is about *returning to your design* — the one that was created to prosper in both spirit and form.

You will not be asked to strive here.
You will not be asked to prove your worth.
You will only be asked to remember it — and to walk like it's true.

You don't have to abandon logic — but you will rise into something greater than it.
You don't have to reject material wealth — you will learn how to receive it without guilt, fear, or grasping.

Here, manifestation is not magic.
It is alignment.
It is truth taking shape.
It is the natural result of living in sync with divine order.

This book will not give you more rules.
It will give you *Laws* — spiritual, universal, living principles that respond not to force, but to faith.

If your soul has been longing for a different way…
If your heart is ready to receive what your mind can't fully plan…
You are in the right place.

This is not the path of striving.
This is the path of remembrance.
And everything changes from here.

You Are Being Remembered

This isn't just a book.

It's a mirror to your essence — a reminder of what you already carry.

You are not broken.

You are not behind.

You are not disqualified.

You are a vessel of infinite supply.

You are being guided home.

Let's begin.

Chapter One

The Law of Divine Inheritance
You Were Born Abundant

This Law is the foundation — the remembrance that you were *born* with access to abundance, not meant to earn it through struggle.

You Were Born Abundant

You were not meant to earn your worth.
You were not sent here to strive for love, security, or approval.

You were designed to *receive*.
To live in harmony with divine flow.
To remember what the world made you forget:

**Before you had a name, before you had a bank account, before anyone told you to be "realistic" —
you were already encoded with wealth.**

Not just potential.
Inheritance.

You are not lacking.
You are not late.
You are not behind.

You are a vessel of divine provision.
And every part of you — even the part that checks the numbers with fear,
scrolling to see how much is left —
is being invited back into truth.

This is not a reward you must earn.
It is your birthright.
And now…
you are remembering.

The Core Teaching

What Is the Law of Divine Inheritance?

The Law of Divine Inheritance is simple, eternal, and often forgotten:

You don't earn abundance — you remember it.

This Law reveals that you are not separate from wealth,
but connected to it by design.
You were not sent here to beg the universe for scraps.
You were created to receive — because you *belong* to the Source of all provision.

The same intelligence that keeps the ocean tides moving, the sun rising, and the trees blooming —
is the same intelligence that formed *you*.

And it didn't send you here without support.

But somewhere along the way, we forgot.

We inherited stories like:

- *"You have to work harder to deserve more."*

- *"Money is earned through pain."*

- *"If I rest, I'll fall behind."*

- *"People like me don't get to live in overflow."*

We inherited guilt.
We inherited lack.
We inherited patterns from families and systems that lived in survival — not because they were wrong, but because they, too, had forgotten.

And so we began to live **as if we were cut off**.
Disconnected.
Alone in the world.
Afraid of what the numbers might say.
Afraid of what happens if the next client doesn't come, the invoice doesn't clear, the door doesn't open.

But the Law says:

You were never disconnected.
You just stopped trusting what you were born to receive.

Divine inheritance is not passive — it is a **posture of remembrance**.
It asks you to:

- Reclaim your identity as a child of the divine
- Realign with the spiritual truth that provision is already in motion
- Release the belief that you must "hustle your way into worthiness"

This is not about sitting back and waiting for miracles.
This is about *walking like you're already supported.*
Because you are.

When you live from this Law, something subtle but powerful begins to happen.

You start making decisions from trust, not tension.
You stop leaking your energy into worry.
You begin to feel — in your body — that you're safe. That you're held. That you can breathe again.

And in that space of inner safety, outer doors open.

Ideas arrive.

People show up.

Opportunities begin to flow — not by chance, but by **design**.

Abundance does not come because you chased it.
It comes because you *returned to your rightful place in the flow.*

Your inheritance is already moving toward you.
Not because you're finally "good enough"…
but because you're starting to remember who you've been all along.

The Story or Insight

The River Doesn't Beg for Water

Imagine a river — wide, alive, flowing.

It doesn't question whether the water will come.
It doesn't ask the sky for permission to be filled.
It doesn't wake up wondering, *"Am I worthy of flow today?"*

The river simply *is*.

It is designed to receive.
To be nourished.
To carry and be carried by something greater than itself.

Now imagine if the river had been taught to hustle.
To dam itself up.
To believe it had to earn every drop.
To feel ashamed every time it overflowed.

Absurd, right?
But that's how most of us live.

You were never meant to beg for what your soul was designed to carry.

We wake up afraid of being too much or not enough.
We try to control the flow with tight fists and tired hearts.
We believe we must suffer to be blessed.
We block the very thing we were born to receive.

But the truth is:
You were created like the river.
Not to chase abundance — but to *channel it*.

You were never meant to beg for what your soul was designed to carry.

And every time you return to this truth —
every time you soften, trust, breathe, let go —
you become available again.

Available to the divine inheritance that has never stopped flowing toward you.

Maybe You Know This Feeling

Maybe you're used to checking your bank account with a quiet ache in your chest.

Not just because the number is low —
but because of what that number has come to mean.

"You're failing."
"You're behind."
"You're not supported."

Even when you believe in abundance…
Even when you try to manifest, pray, visualize…
Some part of you still feels like you have to earn it.
Fix yourself first.
Get everything right before you're allowed to receive.

But let this be, today, your interruption:

You don't have to prove anything to receive what is already yours.
You are not separate from abundance — you are part of it.

You're not winning the lottery today.
You're not landing a miracle client in the next five minutes.

But something inside you is softening.
You are exhaling.
You're saying yes to rest.
You're making a choice from faith, not fear.

And the flow is beginning to return.

Not all at once —
but enough to feel it again.
Enough to remember it was never gone.
Only blocked.

You're remembering now
that you are allowed to be carried by it.

Living the Law

How to Apply the Law of Divine Inheritance in Your Daily Life

Living this Law doesn't require a perfect mindset or a spiritual breakthrough.
It begins in ordinary moments — where fear used to lead, and now, trust starts to speak.

You might notice yourself:

- **Taking a deep breath before checking your balance** — choosing regulation over panic, presence over spiraling

- **Saying no to something that drains you** — even when it's uncomfortable, because you know alignment is more powerful than approval

- **Choosing rest** — not because you "earned it," but because your worth isn't something to prove

- **Asking, "What would I do if I knew I was already supported?"** — and letting that answer lead your next step

These aren't grand gestures.
They're quiet acts of reclamation.
And each one whispers: *I remember.*

Let This In: Journal with Compassion

Journaling is a conversation between your soul and your awareness.
It's where hidden beliefs surface.
It's where clarity is born.
It's where healing begins — not through force, but through gentle observation.

You don't need to write the "right" answers.
You only need to be honest.
Let this be a space where nothing is judged, and everything is welcome.

Reflect on these:

- Where in my life am I still trying to **earn** what is already mine?

- What did I learn about worth or wealth that I'm ready to unlearn?

- If I deeply believed I was already supported... what would I do differently today?

Speak the Truth: Affirmations of Alignment

Affirmations are not empty words.
They are seeds of truth, spoken into the soil of your subconscious.

Each time you say them, you are choosing to align with a deeper reality —
even if your outer world hasn't caught up yet.

Say them softly or boldly, in stillness or in motion.
Let them become a rhythm. A remembering.

I am a vessel of divine abundance.
I don't earn my inheritance — I remember it.
I am safe to receive what is already mine.
My provision flows from alignment, not effort.
I walk as one who is supported.

Say them until they feel like home.

Journaling and affirmations aren't just nice ideas… they're **spiritual technology** — designed to rewire your mind, regulate your body, and realign your life with truth.

Final Whisper

You are not behind.
You are not broken.
You are not missing the secret key.

You are already inside the flow.

Not because you mastered the mindset.
Not because you got every step right.
But because you *belong* to it.
You always have.

Every time you rest… you realign.
Every time you breathe… you soften control.
Every time you trust, even just a little… the current carries you.

You don't have to fight to be worthy.
You don't have to prove you deserve more.
You just have to remember:

You are already connected.
You are already allowed.
You are already chosen.

So let this be your quiet revolution:
To stop earning what's already yours —
and start living like someone who was born abundant.

The flow hasn't forgotten you.
And now… neither have you.

Chapter Two

The Law of Belief and Perception
You Receive What You Believe

This Law is about the inner lens that shapes everything: how your subconscious beliefs become the blueprint for your outer reality. Not as punishment — but as a mirror.

Your beliefs are not just thoughts. They are creators.
They don't describe your life — they design it.

You Receive What You Believe

You are not experiencing life as it is —
you are experiencing life as *you believe it to be.*

Your perception is not passive.
It is a projector.

Your beliefs are not background noise —
they are building the structure of your reality,
brick by invisible brick.

If you believe you are alone,
you will overlook every sign that you are being carried.

If you believe abundance is limited,
you will close the door before it even knocks.

But when you begin to believe something new —
not perfectly, but *bravely* —
the world begins to reflect it.

Not because you forced it,
but because **you became a match for what was already true.**

The Core Teaching

What Is the Law of Belief and Perception?

This Law reveals one of the most overlooked truths of abundance:

You are not responding to reality — you are shaping it.
Not from ego, but from energy.
Not from logic, but from belief.

Every thought you hold long enough to feel,
every story you tell yourself repeatedly,
every silent expectation you carry —
becomes a lens through which life must appear.

This is not punishment.
This is **spiritual physics**.

The universe is not judging you.
It is simply reflecting you.
It is saying, *"As you believe, so shall it be done unto you."*

If you believe money only comes through struggle,
you will unconsciously reject ease.
If you believe your success threatens others,
you'll dim your light before you even speak.
If you believe you're not worthy of overflow,
you will sabotage or shrink every time it tries to find you.

And here's the hardest part:
Most of your beliefs are hidden.
Buried deep in the subconscious.
Shaped by childhood, culture, religion, trauma, and repetition.

But this Law is not here to shame you — it's here to *empower* you.

Because here's the shift:

Your beliefs are not permanent.
They can be rewritten.
They can be healed.
And as they change — *everything changes with them.*

This is why mindset work, spiritual alignment, and inner healing matter.
Because you don't manifest what you *want* —
you manifest what you *believe is possible, available, and safe* to receive.

To unlock abundance, you don't need to force reality to change.
You need to change the lens you're looking through.

When you believe in overflow,
you start to notice opportunities you used to overlook.
You start to trust timing instead of panicking.
You make different choices — not from fear, but from vision.

And the universe responds — not to your words,
but to your *energetic permission slip*.

The Story or Insight

The Mirror You Forgot Was Yours

Imagine standing in front of a mirror,
but instead of seeing your reflection, you see a scene from your life:

A bill left unpaid.
An opportunity missed.
A closed door.
A job that drains you.
An account that never seems to grow.

And every day, you stare at that mirror and think,
"This is who I am."
"This is just how life is."

But what you don't realize is —
you're not looking into a mirror.
You're looking into a **projection** of your past beliefs.
You're seeing not what's fixed, but what you've come to expect.

It's like wearing colored lenses without knowing it.
If your glasses are tinted gray,
even the sunniest day will look dull.
If you believe life is hard, love is rare, or money only comes with pain —
you won't see possibility even when it's right in front of you.

But what happens when you remember the lens is not truth — it's just programming?

You begin to take the glasses off.
You begin to question the voice that says,
"This is all you get."
"You're not the kind of person abundance finds."

And suddenly…
the mirror begins to reflect something different.
Not because the world changed —
but because **you did.**

Belief is the brush.
Perception is the paint.
Your reality is the canvas.

When you shift the inner image,
you don't just imagine a new life —
you begin to *walk into it*.

Maybe You've Done This Without Realizing

Maybe you've said things like:

- "I'm just not good with money."
- "Things like that never happen for me."
- "I'd love to, but that's not realistic."
- "People like me don't get to live like that."

And in the moment, it feels true.
It feels like you're just naming what *is*.

But pause with compassion — what if you weren't describing reality?
What if you were **repeating a belief that's been shaping it?**

This is not blame.
This is power.

Because if a belief built it,
a new belief can transform it.

What you see today may be real —
but it is *not final*.
Your perception is not a life sentence.
It is a canvas waiting for a new vision.

And the shift begins the moment you say:

"What if I believed something different?"

Living the Law

How to Apply the Law of Belief and Perception in Your Daily Life

Your beliefs are not just thoughts —
they're instructions to the Universe.
And the good news is: they can be rewritten.

Living this Law doesn't mean pretending you never doubt.
It means learning to **notice the stories you've been carrying**,
and choosing which ones you want to keep.

You might begin to catch yourself saying:

- "I never have enough."
- "That's not realistic for me."
- "I always mess this up."

And instead of letting those thoughts run on autopilot,
you pause — and ask:

"Is this belief creating the life I want?"

That pause is where the shift begins.
It's how the old lens begins to fall away.

Let This In: Journal with Compassion

Journaling is how you hold space for truth to rise.

It lets the unconscious become seen — not judged, just witnessed.
And in that witnessing, healing begins.

Reflect on these:

- What beliefs about money, success, or self-worth have I inherited without choosing?

- Which of these beliefs have I repeated so often they've become "truth"?

- What would I love to believe instead — even if I don't fully believe it yet?

Let yourself be honest.
This is not about fixing.
It's about becoming aware.

Speak the Truth: Affirmations of Clarity and Power

Affirmations are not positive fluff.
They are **energetic instructions** that reshape your perception and identity.
Even if your current reality hasn't changed yet — speaking truth *aligns you* with what's possible.

Say these aloud. Feel the vibration. Let them plant something new.

I am rewriting my reality with truth.
I see through the eyes of possibility.
I release the beliefs that no longer serve my abundance.
My perception is a portal to overflow.
I am safe to believe in more.

Embodiment Practice: A Moment of Rewiring

Pick one moment today when an old belief shows up — even something subtle, like "I can't afford that" or "I'm not ready."

Pause.

Close your eyes.
Take a breath.
And ask yourself:

"What belief would serve the future I desire?"

Then, speak it. Or write it down.
Not because you have to force a new reality,
but because you're choosing a new lens.

This is how alignment becomes action.
This is how perception becomes power.

Final Whisper

Your reality is not a punishment.
It's a reflection —
of what you've believed,
of what you've expected,
of what you've allowed to be repeated.

But now, you are waking up.
You are seeing the lens for what it is —
and realizing you can choose a new one.

The Universe is not waiting on perfection.
It's waiting on permission.

Believe in something greater,
even before you see it —
and life will begin to rise to meet you.

Chapter Three

The Law of Worthiness

You Receive What You Believe You Deserve

This chapter is all about **deservingness** — the *emotional gate* of abundance. Because even if someone believes abundance exists… if they don't believe they're worthy of it, they'll unconsciously reject it.

You Receive What You Believe You Deserve

Abundance doesn't ask,
"Have you worked hard enough?"
"Have you suffered enough?"
"Have you earned this yet?"

It asks one quiet question:

"Do you believe you are worthy of receiving?"

You can believe in miracles —
but if you feel unworthy, you'll block the door.
You can desire wealth —
but if you feel guilty receiving, you'll shrink it as soon as it comes.

This Law does not punish.
It reveals.

Because life will always mirror what you believe you deserve.

And the moment you remember your true worth —
the flow begins again.

The Core Teaching

What Is the Law of Worthiness?

The Law of Worthiness reveals one of the greatest spiritual misunderstandings of our time:

Abundance is not earned. It is received in proportion to what you believe you deserve.

This is why people with massive potential stay stuck.
Why talented, kind, brilliant souls block their own overflow.
Why even those who believe in abundance never fully let it in.

Because underneath it all, something whispers:
"Not yet."
"Not me."
"Not until I'm better."

Most people don't consciously think they're unworthy.
But they feel it in small, quiet ways:

- They undercharge or overgive
- They deflect compliments
- They apologize for taking up space
- They sabotage blessings that arrive "too easily"

And when the blessing leaves, they say, *"See? I knew it wouldn't last."*

But the problem wasn't the blessing —
it was the belief.

Worthiness is the **energetic gatekeeper** of abundance.

It's the internal "yes" that tells life,
"I'm available for more."

Not in arrogance — in alignment.

Because here's the truth most of us were never told:

You don't become worthy.
You *are* worthy — because you exist.
The question is not whether you've earned it.
The question is whether you'll allow it.

This Law reminds us that receiving is not selfish.
It's sacred.

Your worth doesn't increase when you sacrifice more, struggle more, or prove yourself to others.
It becomes visible when you finally stop arguing with your own enoughness.

When you stop shrinking.
Stop disqualifying yourself.
Stop treating your desires like they need to be justified.

And instead — you rise.
You receive.
You trust.

Not because you're "ready"…
but because **you are already worthy.**

The Story or Insight

The Locked Door With Your Name On It

Imagine a beautiful room filled with every kind of abundance —
peace, wealth, opportunity, love, ease.
It's already been prepared for you.
It even has your name on the door.

But the door won't open with effort.
It won't open with hustle.
It won't open with shame.

It opens when you believe you're allowed to walk in.

And that's the part no one taught you:
The room was never locked from the outside.
It was your own unworthiness turning the handle the wrong way.

You can stand outside the room your whole life,
peeking through the windows, watching others walk in,
thinking they must be more gifted, more prepared, more chosen.

But they're not.
They've simply said yes to what they believe they're allowed to receive.

It's not the Universe keeping you out.
It's the belief that you're not enough to walk in.

That belief might not shout — it whispers:

- *"Be grateful for what you have."*
- *"Don't be greedy."*
- *"People like you don't get that kind of life."*

So you shrink what you ask for.
You apologize for your desires.
You limit the vision, not because it's unrealistic —
but because *you don't believe you're allowed to have it.*

But the door is still there.
And it has never once asked for proof of your worth —
only your permission to receive.

Worthiness is not earned through effort.
It is claimed through remembrance.
You don't unlock abundance by being perfect —
You unlock it by deciding:

"I no longer argue with my own enoughness."

That's the moment the door opens.

Maybe You've Felt This Before

You receive a gift, and your first instinct is to shrink.
You get praised — and immediately downplay it.
Money arrives, and you feel guilty for how "easy" it came.
You say *"thank you"* with your words, but *"I don't deserve this"* with your energy.

This is what unworthiness sounds like.
Not as loud shame, but as subtle contraction.
As emotional flinching.
As hesitation when life tries to bless you.

But here's the truth:

Worthiness isn't a reward for being perfect.
It's a remembering of what's always been true.

You don't need to earn your place at the table.
You need to stop sitting at the edge, apologizing for your hunger.

Living the Law

How to Apply the Law of Worthiness in Your Daily Life

Unworthiness doesn't always sound like shame.
Sometimes it sounds like being "reasonable."
Like always choosing what's practical, not what's aligned.
Like saying yes to less, even when your soul is asking for more.

Living this Law means listening closely to the moments you shrink —
not to judge yourself, but to awaken.

You might notice:

- You hesitate before asking for what you truly want
- You tone yourself down to keep others comfortable
- You undercharge, overgive, or apologize for your success
- You receive something beautiful… and immediately feel guilty

These are the places where unworthiness hides.
Not to punish you — but to show you where the healing is ready.

Every time you choose to honor your desire, your value, your enoughness —
you're not being selfish.
You're practicing **alignment**.

And life meets you there.

Let This In: Journal with Compassion

Journaling is how we sit with what's been hiding under the surface.
It gives the silent parts of us a voice — and turns awareness into freedom.

Let these prompts be a mirror, not a test:

- Where in my life do I still feel I have to "deserve" good things?
- What was I taught about humility, sacrifice, or earning love?
- What do I deeply want… that I've been afraid to claim?

Let honesty rise. Let judgment fall away.
This is where the unlearning begins.

Speak the Truth: Affirmations of Enoughness

Affirmations are a way of rewriting the subconscious script.
They don't just add new thoughts — they **dismantle old lies.**

Speak these aloud. Let your body hear them.
Say them even if they feel unfamiliar — especially then.

I am enough, exactly as I am.
I don't have to earn what is already mine.
I allow myself to receive with peace and joy.
I no longer apologize for my abundance.
My worth is not up for negotiation.

Say them until they feel like your baseline.

Embodiment Practice: Say Yes to What You Once Shrunk

Today, notice one moment when you're tempted to minimize yourself:
to say no when you want to say yes,
to settle for "fine" when your soul is asking for *more*.

Pause.
Take a breath.
And choose worthiness.

That might mean:

- Naming your desire out loud
- Making the bold ask you've been avoiding
- Allowing yourself to take up space in a room, a conversation, or a decision
- Resting, receiving, or raising your standard — without explanation

One brave yes to yourself is a message to the Universe:
"I no longer reject what was always mine."

Final Whisper

You were never meant to beg for your blessings.
Never meant to shrink your desires to make others more comfortable.
Never meant to prove your worth through exhaustion or perfection.

You were born worthy.
You have always been worthy.
And nothing you've walked through has changed that.

The flow you seek is waiting.
Not for you to become more —
but for you to finally say yes to who you already are.

The moment you stop apologizing for your enoughness, the door opens.
And it opens wide.

Chapter Four

The Law of Alignment

When You Align with Truth, You Align with Abundance

This chapter is the bridge between *inner belief* and *outer flow*.

When You Align with Truth, You Align with Abundance

Abundance isn't a prize you chase.
It's a frequency you align with.
A rhythm you remember.
A flow you return to.

There is no need to force what is meant for you.
What you're seeking is already in motion —
but it flows along the current of truth, not fear.

When you align with who you really are,
what you truly value,
what your soul came here to express —
you become magnetic.

Doors open.
Resources flow.
Life begins to meet you with grace.

The more aligned you are,
the less you have to force.
And the more you allow.

The Core Teaching

What Is the Law of Alignment?

The Law of Alignment teaches a profound and liberating truth:

You don't manifest by force — you manifest by frequency.

When your thoughts, actions, energy, and identity are aligned with truth,
you become a clear signal for abundance.
You stop chasing.
You start attracting.
You stop striving.
You start receiving.

Not because life suddenly "likes you" —
but because you've stopped sending mixed signals to the Universe.

Most people don't struggle because they're unworthy.
They struggle because they're *out of alignment*.

They want ease, but stay loyal to stress.
They want overflow, but keep choosing scarcity.
They say they trust, but make decisions from fear.

And the Universe — always responsive, always listening —
meets them in their contradiction.

You can't live out of alignment and expect aligned results.

This is not judgment.
This is law.

Alignment is not about perfection.
It's about *resonance*.

It's when who you are, what you say, what you choose, and how you move
all begin to match.

It's when your nervous system relaxes into truth,
and your actions rise from faith instead of fear.

It's when you stop performing, forcing, or proving —
and start allowing, trusting, and responding.

Here's what happens when you're in alignment:

- You make bold decisions that don't drain you
- You attract opportunities without chasing them
- You feel peace *before* the outcome
- You don't need to control every detail — because your energy is already working for you

You start walking in a new rhythm.
You start making choices that echo your inner knowing.
And in that place — abundance meets you naturally.

Alignment is not something you do once.
It's a way of living that tunes you to the divine flow.

The Story or Insight

The Sound of Alignment

Imagine a grand piano — beautiful, powerful, full of potential.

But even the most exquisite instrument,
if even a single string is out of tune,
will produce a sound that feels… off.

No matter how skilled the pianist is,
no matter how expensive the room,
the music can't move you unless it's *in tune*.

This is how many people live:
Doing all the right things.
Saying the right words.
Working hard. Visualizing. Hoping.

But something inside feels… dissonant.

That dissonance isn't failure.
It's feedback.

It's the body saying,
"This choice doesn't match what I truly want."
"This job doesn't honor who I really am."
"This relationship, this pace, this pressure — it's not aligned with truth."

And when you're out of alignment, everything feels harder.

You push.
You chase.
You perform.
You make decisions from fear, and call it responsibility.
You feel the exhaustion of trying to create results with energy that doesn't match your intention.

But when you realign — even slightly —
the dissonance disappears.

You say the true yes.
You take the brave no.
You speak more honestly.
You move at your soul's pace.
You begin to live in harmony.

And suddenly… the music changes.

Alignment doesn't guarantee a perfect life — but it does return you to your *natural rhythm*.
The place where peace lives.
The place where abundance flows.

Maybe You've Felt This Before

Maybe you've said yes when you meant no —
because you didn't want to disappoint anyone.

Maybe you stayed too long in something that drained you —
a job, a pace, a pattern — because it felt "safe."

Maybe you've had an intuitive nudge,
a moment of deep knowing…
and you overrode it in favor of logic or fear.

You were in motion — but out of tune.

This is what misalignment feels like:

- Waking up tired even after rest
- Earning money but feeling disconnected from purpose
- Achieving things that don't feel like you

- Making decisions that look right on paper but feel wrong in your body

It doesn't always look like chaos.
Sometimes it just feels… off.

But that *off* is the invitation.
Not to do more — but to realign.

You don't have to blow up your life to come back into harmony.
You only need to start choosing truth — one aligned yes at a time.

Living the Law

How to Apply the Law of Alignment in Your Daily Life

Alignment isn't a mood — it's a relationship.
With your truth.
With your body.
With the divine.

You may be out of alignment if:

- You keep saying yes to things that drain you
- You're successful but not satisfied
- You're busy, but not clear
- You feel constant pressure to force outcomes

Alignment feels different.

When you're aligned:

- Decisions feel clean
- You rest without guilt
- You act from peace, not panic
- You feel deeply honest with yourself — and deeply supported by life

The path doesn't become perfect.
But it becomes *clear*.

Let This In: Journal with Compassion

Journaling helps you hear what your spirit has been trying to say.

Let these prompts be a sacred pause — a space to notice what's true.

- What in my life currently feels "off" — even if it looks good on the outside?
- Where am I making choices out of fear, obligation, or habit?
- What would it look like to move in the direction of deeper alignment?

Don't rush your answers.
Let your body speak, too.

Speak the Truth: Affirmations of Alignment

Affirmations help you come back into harmony —
not by forcing belief, but by *tuning yourself back to truth*.

Speak these aloud. Feel their resonance.

I am safe to move in alignment with my soul.
I no longer force what's not meant for me.
I release urgency and trust divine timing.
My energy is most powerful when I'm aligned.
I give myself permission to choose what's true.

Embodiment Practice: Follow the Spark of Truth

Today, choose **just one small action** that honors what feels aligned — even if it's small.

You don't need to change everything.
You just need to move one step closer to what's true.

Here's what alignment might look like in real life:

- **At work:** You speak up about a boundary or request a change that better supports your energy

- **In your relationships:** You lovingly say no to something that doesn't feel right — or yes to something you've been avoiding out of fear

- **In your time:** You cancel or postpone something that's only on your calendar out of obligation, not resonance

- **In your body:** You pause and check in — *"Does this choice feel tight or clear?"* — and let your next step reflect that

It doesn't have to be perfect.
It just has to be honest.

This is how you realign — not with pressure, but with presence.

Final Whisper

You were never meant to force what's not meant for you.
You were never meant to abandon your truth for acceptance,
approval, or safety.

You were created to move in harmony with the divine —
not with pressure, but with presence.
Not with striving, but with resonance.

When you begin to choose alignment over fear,
you unlock a life that was already waiting for you.

Let it be honest.
Let it be gentle.
Let it be true.

Because in truth, you are already aligned with everything you seek.

Chapter Five

The Law of Divine Timing

The Flow Is Always Right on Time

This chapter is a deep exhale — a spiritual release from pressure, forcing, impatience, and fear of missing out. It's about learning to trust the rhythm *beneath* the waiting.

The Flow Is Always Right on Time

There is a rhythm beneath everything.
A divine unfolding you cannot always see —
but you are always inside of.

You are not late.
You are not behind.
You are not being ignored.

The delay is not a denial —
it's a recalibration.

When it hasn't shown up yet,
it's not because you're doing something wrong.
It's because life is still rearranging things to meet you in the highest way.

The Universe does not rush —
because it does not doubt.

So neither should you.

The Core Teaching

What Is the Law of Divine Timing?

The Law of Divine Timing reminds us:

There is an intelligent rhythm to your life — and you are never outside of it.

Even in the waiting.
Even in the silence.
Even in the seasons that make no sense.

Your life is not random.
It is being orchestrated with precision and love.
You are being led — even when you feel lost.

But here's what most people get wrong:

They think Divine Timing means they should be passive.
That they just have to wait and hope things "work out."

Or... they swing the other way —
and believe that if things aren't flowing, they must be doing something wrong.

The truth is: **it's both.**

You are always inside the divine plan.
But your alignment — your energy, your trust, your choices — shapes how you *move through it*.

If you try to force what's not ready, you create resistance.
If you act from fear, the doors may stay closed — not to punish you, but to protect what you're not ready to hold.

If you try to outrun the process, you may miss the very step that leads to the breakthrough.

But none of that means you're failing.
Because Divine Timing is merciful.
It folds your detours into the map.
It uses your delays as preparation.
It recalibrates every time you realign.

You can't miss what's truly meant for you —
but you can **delay your experience of it** when you're out of sync with your own truth.

Alignment doesn't change whether the timing exists —
it changes how you experience it.

And here's something essential to understand:

If someone never experiences the wealth, love, or peace they long for —
it's *not* because it wasn't meant for them.
It's because they may have never felt safe enough, worthy enough, or empowered enough
to receive what was always available.

Not because the Universe withheld it —
but because they were never shown how to align with it.

Abundance is not selective.
It's responsive.

You're not excluded.
You're being invited — again and again — to return to the version of you
who can open the door and *hold* what's been waiting.

And you can.
You're not too far gone.
You haven't missed your moment.
Everything you desire is still alive — because *you're still alive.*
And if you're reading this, the unfolding has already begun.

The invitation is open.
The rhythm is waiting.
And this is your time.

When you align with your flow,
you are always right on time.

This is Divine Timing:
Not a delay.
Not a test.
A dance.

And the moment you stop pushing against the rhythm —
you remember how to move with it.

The Story or Insight

The Seed That Knows When to Bloom

Imagine planting a seed.

You water it.
You nourish the soil.
You check every day to see if it's broken through the surface.

But for a while — there's nothing.
No sprout. No sign. Just dirt.

And you start to wonder:
Did it work?
Did I do something wrong?
Should I dig it up and start over?

But beneath the surface, the seed is moving.
Splitting. Rooting. Stretching.
Doing the invisible work required to one day bloom.

You don't rush a seed because you're in a hurry.
You trust the process because you believe in the design.

Divine Timing works the same way.

Just because you can't see the results
doesn't mean nothing is happening.
Just because you've waited
doesn't mean you've failed.

Life is still working.
And your roots are still growing.

The timeline you imagined isn't a failure.
It's a doorway — to deeper trust, deeper clarity, and better outcomes than you could've scripted.

Maybe You've Felt This Before

Maybe you've been doing the inner work —
changing your mindset, opening your heart,
taking small steps toward the life you desire…

But nothing seems to be "happening."

You keep checking the external for signs:
the number in your account, the call that hasn't come,
the thing that still hasn't shifted.

And some part of you begins to whisper:
"Maybe it's not working."
"Maybe I missed it."
"Maybe I'm not meant for this."

But that voice is just fear trying to fill the silence.

The truth is:

Divine Timing doesn't speak in rush or panic.
It speaks in rhythm.
And right now, something is moving — even if you can't see it yet.

Your only job is to stay in the soil.
To stay in trust.
To stay in alignment.

Because when it's time —
your life will bloom.
And it won't be late.

Living the Law

How to Apply the Law of Divine Timing in Your Daily Life

We live in a world obsessed with speed.
With instant results, constant progress, visible success.
But Divine Timing doesn't obey urgency — it follows *alignment*.

You may be out of sync with Divine Timing if:

- You're constantly checking for "proof" that things are working

- You feel frantic, like you need to hurry before the door closes

- You judge your timeline by someone else's progress

- You push decisions out of fear of missing out

But when you align with the rhythm beneath the rush:

- You make peace with the pace of your life

- You stop mistaking stillness for failure

- You start trusting what's *becoming*, not just what's already visible

- You breathe deeper — even in the waiting

Waiting doesn't mean nothing is happening.
It means everything is preparing.

Let This In: Journal with Compassion

Use these questions to let clarity rise.

You don't have to find the right answers.
You just have to let yourself be *honest*.

- Where in my life am I rushing out of fear or comparison?
- What might life be protecting or preparing me for in this season of delay?
- What would it feel like to trust that what I desire is already on its way?

There's no shame in wanting things to happen faster.
But there's so much freedom in learning to *trust the unfolding*.

Speak the Truth: Affirmations of Trust

Affirmations realign your energy with the deeper rhythm of truth.

Speak them slowly.
Let them soften the edges of impatience.

I trust the timing of my life.
What I seek is seeking me — and will arrive on time.
I am no longer rushing to prove, perform, or control.
I surrender my timeline to divine intelligence.
I move in rhythm with what is real and right for me.

Let them sink in like medicine.
Especially when doubt wants to take over.

Embodiment Practice: Release the Rush

Today, notice where you feel hurried — and gently choose a slower, more trusting rhythm.

Here are a few ways Divine Timing might look in your real life:

- **In your work:** You stop forcing a decision and give it space to become clear

- **In your body:** You go for a walk, take a breath, or slow your pace instead of powering through

- **In your mind:** You stop replaying the "what ifs" and ask, *"What if it's all on time?"*

- **In your heart:** You offer yourself grace for being in process — not finished, but *becoming*

When you stop rushing, you start receiving.
The miracle may not come faster —
but your heart will be ready when it arrives.

Final Whisper

There is nothing wrong with your pace.
There is nothing wrong with your path.
There is nothing wrong with your process.

You are not behind.
You are not missing it.
You are not being punished.

You are being prepared.
You are being positioned.
You are being aligned with something even better than you imagined.

Trust the pauses.
Trust the detours.
Trust the rhythm that lives beneath your plans.

Because the moment you stop rushing to get there —
you realize you've been walking with the miracle all along.

And it's bringing you home.
Right. On. Time.

Chapter Six

The Law of Embodiment
You Become What You Practice

This chapter is where you realize:

Spiritual truth must become lived truth.
It's not just what you believe — it's what you embody.
You create with your energy, your choices, your daily rhythm.

This is where we go from vision → integration → expression.

You Become What You Practice

You don't manifest what you want —
you manifest what you *are*.

Not just what you believe in theory,
but what you embody in practice.

Abundance responds to energy, not effort.
And your energy is shaped by what you practice — in thought, in choice, in presence.

You can know the truth and still live from fear.
You can speak the affirmations and still act from scarcity.

Embodiment is the bridge.

It's how you take spiritual truth out of the clouds
and bring it into your body, your breath, your behavior.

It's not about being perfect —
it's about being *congruent*.

The Core Teaching

What Is the Law of Embodiment?

The Law of Embodiment teaches this simple, powerful truth:

You create from your state — not just your thoughts.
Not from what you say you believe,
but from what your nervous system, your energy, and your choices are *actually practicing.*

Most people know what they desire:
Peace. Overflow. Confidence. Freedom.

But if their daily habits, emotions, posture, and decisions are rehearsing fear, self-doubt, guilt, or lack —
that's what they're embodying.
And that's what gets reflected back.

This isn't about blame — it's about power.

You're not being punished for being inconsistent.
But the Universe *does* respond to your energetic baseline.

If your body still flinches every time you receive,
if your choices reflect fear of loss more than trust in provision,
if your yeses are rooted in pleasing instead of alignment —
then abundance gets confused.
Because you're sending mixed signals.

Embodiment is the point where your identity, energy, and actions come into alignment.

It's when truth becomes natural.
When your choices match your clarity.

When you no longer have to convince yourself — because you *are* it now.

You don't "practice abundance" just in your meditations.
You practice it in:

- The way you hold your posture
- The way you make decisions
- The boundaries you set
- The way you speak, walk, rest, and show up in spaces
- The quiet moments when no one is watching but your soul

The life you're calling in isn't just waiting for your belief.
It's waiting for your embodiment.

Every time you act from the version of you who *already has it*,
you bring that reality closer.

You don't manifest by chasing the future —
you manifest by *becoming* the frequency now.

And the beautiful part?

You don't have to do it all at once.
Embodiment doesn't require perfection.
It only requires *consistency*.

Small shifts.
Repeated.
With presence.

That's the Law of Embodiment.

The Story or Insight

The Mirror That Doesn't Lie

Imagine standing in front of a mirror, holding a script.

You've memorized the lines: "I trust abundance."
"I am enough."
"Money flows to me with ease."

You say them clearly. You even believe them… in your mind.

But your shoulders are tight.
Your breath is shallow.
Your stomach clenches when you open your banking app.
You nod yes when your body is screaming no.
You give when you're empty — and call it generosity.

And the mirror doesn't reflect the words.
It reflects the *state*.

Because life responds to what you *are*, not just what you say.

This is the power of embodiment — and the cost of bypassing it.

You can know all the spiritual laws.
You can say all the right affirmations.
You can visualize every day.

But if your nervous system is rehearsing fear…
If your habits still reflect scarcity…
If your choices are still made from guilt or survival…

Then you're not in resonance — and you won't feel the flow.

Embodiment is when you stop performing belief —
and start living like it's true.

Not as a performance.
Not as a test.
As a quiet congruence between what you believe… and how you breathe.

Maybe You've Felt This Before

You say you trust the Universe…
But you check your phone 15 times for proof.
You believe in rest…
But you still feel guilty when you take a day off.
You say you're worthy of more…
But you still shrink around people who have it.

That's not failure — it's a mirror.

It's showing you where your mind and your body haven't caught up yet.
Where truth is still an idea — not a lived experience.

But here's the gift:

You don't need to wait until everything is perfect to practice the future now.

You just need to take the next step from your *next self*.
Not who you've been…
but who you're becoming.

And every time you do —
you embody the life that's already reaching for you.

Living the Law

How to Apply the Law of Embodiment in Your Daily Life

You already have spiritual truth inside you.
The question now is: **Are you practicing it with your life?**

Embodiment doesn't require perfection.
It requires congruence.

Where your **words, energy, choices, and actions** begin to reflect the same truth.

You may be *disembodied* from your truth if:

- You say you trust, but act from control
- You say you're abundant, but still choose based on fear
- You say you're worthy, but tolerate relationships, work, or environments that say otherwise
- You say you rest, but feel anxious when you're not producing

When you're *in embodiment*, you feel it.

You breathe deeper.
You take cleaner action.
You say yes with your whole body — or no without guilt.
You move in integrity with who you're becoming.

Let This In: Journal with Compassion

This is the moment to get honest — not harsh.
The goal isn't to be perfect. It's to become *aware*.

Let yourself reflect:

- What spiritual truths do I say I believe... but haven't yet fully practiced?
- In what situations does my body still default to fear or control, even when I "know better"?
- If I trusted I was already the version of me who has what I desire — how would I move today?

Let these questions be a mirror, not a measurement.
You're not behind — you're becoming.

Speak the Truth: Affirmations of Integration

These affirmations are not about forcing belief.
They are about reminding your system — *this is who I am now*.

Speak them with presence. Say them with breath.

I am safe to embody the truth I already know.
I no longer abandon myself for comfort or control.
I act from the frequency I desire — not from the fear I've outgrown.
I don't just believe in abundance. I live it.
I am becoming what I was always meant to be.

Let the words become *your walk*.

Embodiment Practice: Move Like It's Already True

Embodiment means you don't just know abundance —
you *live* it in your breath, your behavior, your body language, and your boundaries.

Here are four ways you can practice alignment today —
not just in your mind, but in motion.

When you pay a bill:
Often, paying a bill feels like a loss or an act of sacrifice, driven by fear of not having enough.

Instead, try viewing the payment as an act of gratitude —
an exchange that honors the value and service you receive.

Choosing generosity over fear here doesn't mean spending recklessly;
it means trusting that money isn't a finite resource to be hoarded.

It's acknowledging that when you invest in your life — with trust and thankfulness —
you activate the flow of abundance rather than block it.

When your body wants to say no — but your mouth wants to say yes:
This is where embodiment meets boundaries.

- Before you speak, pause. Breathe.
- Ask: *"Am I choosing from alignment… or from fear?"*
- Notice your body: does it tense or soften?
- Practice saying no with calm, clarity, and kindness.
- Remind yourself: *"Saying no to what shrinks me is saying yes to the life I'm building."*

Every embodied no is a nervous system reclaiming safety in truth.

When you make a spending decision:
Embodiment doesn't mean spending recklessly —
it means choosing from self-trust, not self-doubt.

- Instead of asking, "What's the cheapest thing I can get away with?"
  ask, *"What feels aligned, respectful to my current resources, and honoring to my future self?"*

- Choose one thing today that reflects *self-worth*, not self-neglect — even if it's small.
  A nourishing meal. A moment of beauty. A "yes" to something that brings ease.

This isn't about stretching beyond what's wise.
It's about upgrading your *relationship* with money —
from survival to sovereignty.
From guilt to grounded trust.

Even a small decision made from alignment
creates energetic coherence with the life you're building.

When you talk about your life, goals, or identity:

- Notice if you minimize, apologize, or shrink.

- Try saying one bold truth aloud — *"I'm growing into something powerful."*

- Speak it even if your voice shakes. Especially then.

Your words calibrate your field.
Speak like someone who believes it's already becoming real.

Embodiment is truth in motion.
The moment you act from who you *already are*,
the future begins to arrive in the present.

Final Whisper

You don't become abundant by wishing.
You become abundant by *walking* in the direction of truth.

You don't need to force it.
You don't need to fake it.
You don't need to be perfect.

You only need to show up — again and again —
as the version of you who already knows what's real.

Let your breath be a statement of trust.
Let your choices reflect who you're becoming.
Let your energy lead before the evidence appears.

Because every time you act from alignment —
you close the gap between the vision and the reality.

You don't have to wait to feel it.

You *are* it now.

Chapter Seven

The Law of Inspired Action
Move When the Soul Says Yes

This Law opens a new phase in your journey — from inner alignment into *outer momentum*. But not from hustle... from harmony.

Move When the Soul Says Yes

You were never meant to force your way into your future.
You were meant to walk with the divine — in rhythm, not in panic.

Inspired action is the movement that flows from truth,
not fear.
Not pressure.
Not proving.

You don't manifest just by visualizing.
You manifest by moving in alignment with what you've seen.

This isn't about doing more —
it's about moving from the *right energy*.

From clarity.
From peace.
From the quiet inner yes that rises like a whisper —
"Now."

The Core Teaching

What Is the Law of Inspired Action?

You've probably heard it before:
"Take action. Make it happen. Hustle for your dreams."

But action alone isn't what creates results.
Energy is the true initiator.
Action simply reveals the state behind it.

You can act from fear and block the flow.
You can act from alignment and unlock the door.

The Law of Inspired Action teaches you this:
You don't manifest by sitting still and wishing —
but you also don't manifest by pushing and forcing.

You manifest when your *energy aligns with truth*
and your *actions reflect that alignment.*

Most people are taking action from anxiety, not inspiration.

They move because they're afraid of being left behind.
They push because they think nothing will happen unless they control it.
They chase because they don't trust what's already theirs.

This isn't action — it's survival dressed as productivity.
It doesn't attract abundance — it repels it.

Because the Universe doesn't just respond to *what* you do...
It responds to *why* you're doing it.

Inspired action is clear, clean, and rooted in peace.
It doesn't drain you — it energizes you.
It doesn't scramble for outcomes — it flows from trust.

It might still be bold. It might stretch you.
But it's not *reactive* — it's *responsive*.

It's not fear disguised as focus.
It's alignment translated into motion.

So how do you know when action is inspired?

- It feels like a *nudge*, not a push
- It often comes with clarity, timing, or a sudden inner yes
- It's backed by trust — not desperation
- It honors your body's wisdom, not your ego's urgency
- And even if it scares you… it comes with peace

This law doesn't ask you to wait forever.
It asks you to **listen** first.
And then — when the call rises — to move.

Because manifestation is a partnership.
And when your soul says yes… the Universe does too.

The Story or Insight

The Arrow That Doesn't Need to Be Pushed

Imagine an arrow.
Its only job is to fly — straight, swift, with purpose.

But the archer doesn't push the arrow forward.
They pull back, anchor, and wait for the right moment.
And then — release.

No striving.
No forcing.
Just the natural momentum that comes from alignment.

This is how inspired action works.

It doesn't come from trying harder.
It comes from being aligned… and then released.

The problem is, most people don't trust the pause.

They act too early — out of panic.
They try to push the arrow with their hands instead of trusting the tension to build.

Or they freeze — afraid to move at all.

But action taken too soon drains you.
Action taken too late deflates you.
Only action taken from *inner clarity* has power.

It might look small from the outside — a call, a yes, a step forward.
But when it comes from alignment, that one step carries *unseen force*.

It's the arrow released from the soul.

Inspired action is not always loud — but it is always precise.
You'll know it by the feeling that follows:
Peace, even in risk.
Clarity, even in uncertainty.
Momentum, without exhaustion.

Maybe You've Felt This Before

You launch something — not because your soul said yes, but because you felt behind.
You say yes to a job, a client, an idea — even though your body felt tight.
You send the message, sign the contract, make the decision —
but it's not from excitement. It's from fear.

And afterward… you feel it.

The drain.
The doubt.
The question: *"Why doesn't this feel right?"*

It's not that you acted — it's *how* you acted.

You moved from misalignment.

But you can choose differently now.

You can wait for the moment when the nudge feels clean.
When your soul is ready.
When peace says: *"Now."*

That's the moment your action becomes a prayer —
and the Universe answers it in motion.

Living the Law

How to Apply the Law of Inspired Action in Your Daily Life

We've been taught to act fast.
To hustle, push, chase, and control.
But **inspired action doesn't come from pressure** — it comes from *presence*.

The question isn't just: *"Am I doing enough?"*
It's: *"Am I doing what my soul is asking me to do — from the right energy?"*

You may be out of alignment with inspired action if:

- You feel urgency, panic, or pressure to act *now* without clarity
- You say yes even when something feels wrong in your body
- You chase results instead of responding to intuition
- You take action because you're afraid of being behind

When action is inspired, it feels different:

- There's often a quiet "yes" before the mind even understands why
- The next step feels natural, clean, and clear — even if it's a stretch
- You feel energized afterward, not depleted
- You trust the timing, even if the outcome isn't instant

Let This In: Journal with Compassion

Use these prompts to clear out noise and connect to your next aligned step:

- Where am I taking action from fear, not faith?
- What is one area of my life where I feel urgency — and what's really underneath it?
- What decision or movement have I been delaying that *actually* feels like a true yes?

Don't try to figure it all out — just listen.
Inspired action often rises in stillness, not strategy.

Speak the Truth: Affirmations of Alignment in Motion

Let these words become your rhythm.
Say them before a big decision… or before your feet hit the floor.

I move when the moment is right — not when fear says go.
I trust that right timing brings right results.
My action is guided, not forced.
I listen before I leap.
I allow inspired momentum to carry me.

Embodiment Practice: Move from the Quiet Yes

Inspired action doesn't always arrive with a thunderclap.
It often whispers.
A tug on your attention.
A moment of quiet clarity in the middle of your day.
A thought that returns again and again, asking to be honored.

Today, choose just one area of your life.
And within that space, choose one step — not from urgency, but from *truth*.

Here's how inspired action might speak to you:

In your work, calling, or purpose:
Maybe you scroll past people making money online —
sharing their voice, building something flexible, free, creative —
and you feel that mix of envy and ache: *"Why them and not me?"*

The truth is: it's not because they're luckier.
It's because they moved.
They gave their desire a chance to take shape.

So today, start there.

- Set aside an hour — not to scroll, but to research. Slowly. Calmly. With intention.
  Explore the spaces that genuinely interest you: writing, design, coaching, e-commerce, content creation, consulting, something of your own.
  Look at what's possible — not with pressure, but with permission.
  Ask: *"What would it look like for me to be part of this?"*

Or maybe you already have a job, but it's draining you.
You feel underpaid. Unseen.
And you've been telling yourself to be grateful —
but some deeper part of you knows: *it's time to move.*

So today, begin the shift.

- Refresh your résumé.

- Reconnect with someone in a field that excites you.

- Look at opportunities not as a fantasy — but as a match for your growth.

- Send one application, even if your inner critic says, "You're not qualified."

- You don't need to be perfect — you need to be present.

The soul doesn't ask for leaps.
It asks for momentum.
One honest move at a time.

In your relationships and connections:
Sometimes the most powerful action is not to achieve — but to *honor your own needs*.

Maybe you've been holding your tongue to keep the peace.
Or tolerating something that no longer fits, because you're afraid to disappoint.

Inspired action might look like finally setting the boundary.
Saying the thing you've been avoiding — but that your body *knows* is true.

Or maybe it's opening instead of closing —
reaching out to someone who feels aligned, even if it's vulnerable.
Letting yourself be seen, without overexplaining.

Truth creates cleaner relationships.
And when you move from truth — not people-pleasing or self-protection —
the right connections will feel lighter, not heavier.

In your relationship with money:
Inspired action in this space often reveals where fear still leads.

Maybe there's a decision you've been avoiding —
canceling the thing that drains you, asking for what you're worth, or spending on something that expands you instead of just "making do."

This isn't about recklessness or magical thinking.
It's about making one financial move from *alignment*, not anxiety.

- You might invest in a tool, a course or teacher that your future self would thank you for.

- Or maybe it's finally canceling a subscription that drains you, and releasing it with peace.

Money responds to clarity.
One clean, conscious action begins to shift your whole energetic pattern.

In your body or creativity:
Your creativity is one of the most sacred channels of divine flow.
And yet, so often we silence it — waiting until we have time, space, a reason, a goal.

But the muse doesn't come because you're ready.
She comes because you *begin*.

Today, listen for the small invitation:

- Dance. Walk. Breathe. Move in a way that reconnects you to your own momentum

- To sit down and create without editing — a sketch, a song, a journal entry

- To do something not because it's "productive," but because it *lights your inner fire*

This isn't about becoming an artist.
It's about honoring the life force that wants to move through you.

One moment of embodied expression can unlock everything that felt stuck.

You don't need to make a bold leap today.
You only need to say yes to the *quiet next step*.
The one that keeps circling back to you.
The one that doesn't demand proof — just permission.

Inspired action is not about force.
It's about resonance.
It's the step that already lives inside your knowing —
waiting for you to let it breathe.

Final Whisper

There will be moments when the way forward is unclear.
When doubt gets louder than direction.
When you'll be tempted to freeze… or to force.

But here is your truth:

You are not here to chase.
You are here to respond —
to clarity, to peace, to timing, to the quiet yes that lives in your body.

The Universe moves when you do.
Not from panic, but from presence.
Not from pressure, but from trust.

You don't need to know the whole plan.
You just need to honor the part that's already whispering:
"This is your next step."

So take it.

Even if it's small.
Even if you're trembling.
Even if the outcome is still a mystery.

Your action is the invitation.
Your trust is the offering.
And the moment you move with the Divine —
the doors begin to open.

Chapter Eight

The Law of Receiving

Let It Come In

This chapter is the sacred *counterbalance* to Inspired Action.
It's not about doing — it's about *letting*.
It's about opening the heart, softening the grip, and learning how to stop blocking what is already trying to arrive.

Let It Come In

You were never meant to only give.
You were meant to receive.

Not just love.
Not just money.
But rest. Support. Beauty. Overflow. Guidance.

The Universe doesn't just respond to your action.
It responds to your *openness*.

You can pray for abundance and still block it.
You can want love and still reject it.
You can ask for a miracle and then push it away when it knocks —
because some part of you still believes you have to earn it.

But receiving isn't a reward.
It's a rhythm.
And you're allowed to let it in.

The Core Teaching

What Is the Law of Receiving?

The Law of Receiving teaches us that **abundance flows not just to those who ask — but to those who are *open*.**

You can do all the inner work...
You can visualize, affirm, align, and act —
but if your energy isn't open to *receive*,
you will block what you've been asking for.

Receiving isn't passive.
It's not sitting back and hoping something good will happen.

Receiving is an energetic posture.
A sacred openness.
A willingness to let life support you — without guilt, without apology, without shrinking.

And for many people... that's the hardest part.

We've been taught to give, give, give —
to serve, to solve, to sacrifice.
But to *receive*?
That's vulnerable.
That means trusting that you don't have to earn everything.
That means letting go of control and letting something good *meet you*.

You may be blocking receiving if:

- You immediately deflect compliments or help
- You feel guilty when things come easily

- You overgive to avoid feeling selfish
- You downplay your desires
- You're constantly in motion — but uncomfortable with stillness

These are not flaws.
They are signs of old survival patterns —
the parts of you that learned it was safer to be in control than to be held.

But you're safe now.

And receiving is your return to that safety —
not as a reward, but as a *remembering*.

When you learn to receive:

- You say thank you — without apology or explanation
- You allow rest, pleasure, and support to nourish you
- You accept blessings with grace, not guilt
- You become a magnet for more, because you're no longer resisting what's already yours

Receiving is not lazy.
It's not selfish.
It's the final, most sacred part of manifestation:

The moment when you say to the Universe —
"I'm ready to hold what I once only hoped for."

The Story or Insight

The Gift You Keep Pushing Away

Imagine someone shows up at your door
with a gift — wrapped beautifully, just for you.

They knock gently.
You peek through the window.
You want what they're holding… but you hesitate.

"What if I don't deserve it?"
"What will they expect from me in return?"
"What if it disappears as soon as I take it?"

So you pretend you're not home.
Or you open the door halfway and say, *"Thank you, but I'm good."*

They leave the gift on the doorstep.
But you never open it.

This is what many of us do with love, with money, with support, with ease.
We ask… but we don't open.

We pray… but we stay braced.
We affirm… but we secretly don't feel worthy.
We take pride in independence — but inwardly long to be held.

Receiving is uncomfortable, because it requires surrender.
It asks us to soften.
To be vulnerable.
To believe we are allowed to be supported, loved, filled, chosen.

But here's the truth:

The gifts are already at your door.
Life is trying to give to you — but it can only enter through open hands.

Maybe You've Felt This Before

Someone offers to help — and your first response is, *"No, I'm fine."*
You get a compliment — and you deflect it.
You receive money — and immediately feel guilty, or try to justify why you deserve it.
You ask for a sign — and then doubt it when it shows up.

This isn't failure. It's just old wiring.
Your body learned to equate receiving with risk.

But receiving is not a threat.
It's a return to trust.
It's how you learn to hold the life you've been calling in.

So this is your practice now:

Let it land.
Let it soften you.
Let the love, the compliment, the support, the money *in*.
Don't analyze it. Don't argue with it.
Just say, *"Thank you. I receive."*

Because you are meant to receive — fully, freely, and without apology.

Living the Law

How to Apply the Law of Receiving in Your Daily Life

Most people think they're waiting to receive.
But in truth, *receiving is waiting for them.*

We pray.
We visualize.
We work hard.
But when the blessings come… we deflect them, doubt them, or downplay them.

Not because we don't want to receive —
but because we've been conditioned to believe that we have to **earn** it all first.

You don't receive what you ask for.
You receive what you *allow yourself to hold.*

You might be resisting receiving if:

- You feel awkward or unworthy when someone gives to you

- You only feel valuable when you're the one helping, doing, giving

- You immediately try to "balance the scale" when someone offers support or money

- You say things like, *"I'm fine,"* *"It's too much,"* or *"You don't have to…"*

- You reject stillness and softness because it feels unproductive or indulgent

These are learned patterns — not your truth.

The truth is:
You are allowed to receive simply because you exist.
You are allowed to be filled, supported, and seen.
You are allowed to say yes to good things *without guilt*.

Let This In: Journal with Compassion

Receiving begins with **awareness** — not force.

Use these prompts to gently uncover where you've been blocking the flow:

- Where in my life do I find it hard to receive?

- What story am I still holding about needing to "earn" what I desire?

- What would it feel like to receive — without guilt, without shrinking, without apology?

Let your answers be honest and soft.
You are not broken. You are learning to open.

Speak the Truth: Affirmations of Worth and Openness

Say them slowly.
Let each line sink into the places that once resisted.

I am open to receiving what I've already asked for.
I don't have to earn what is already mine.
I release guilt and welcome grace.
I trust that I am worthy of support, love, and abundance — without overgiving to prove it.
It is safe to let the good land.

Embodiment Practice: Let Something Land Today

Today, receive something *on purpose*.

It might be a compliment, an offer of help, a payment, a sign, a moment of ease —
but instead of brushing it off or minimizing it…
let it in.

And let it be *enough*.

Here are some simple ways to practice:

- **When someone gives you a compliment:** pause. Don't deflect. Just breathe it in and say, *"Thank you. I receive that."*

- **When money comes in (even a small amount):** maybe someone pays for your coffee. Maybe a friend covers lunch. Maybe you're gifted something you would've normally paid for.

    Whatever form it takes, don't brush it off. Smile. Acknowledge it. Feel gratitude not just for the money — but for your capacity to *receive* it.

- **When you feel tired:** rest. Let rest be an act of receiving, not something you have to earn.

- **When someone offers help or support:** say yes — even if you could technically do it yourself.

This is how you train your nervous system to recognize support as safe.
This is how you tell the Universe, *"I'm available now."*

Let something in today — not because you need it,
but because you are worthy of it.

Final Whisper

You don't have to brace anymore.
You don't have to prove.
You don't have to earn what was already meant for you.

There is a version of you that trusts the opening.
That says thank you without shrinking.
That lets the good land — and lets it stay.

Receiving is not weakness.
It is the quiet power of a soul that knows its worth.

So let it in.
The compliment.
The support.
The ease.
The miracle.

Don't argue with it.
Don't minimize it.
Don't hand it back.

Just say,
"I receive."

And watch what flows in when your hands are open.

Chapter Nine

The Law of Circulation
What Flows Through You, Grows With You

This chapter is about movement — the divine rhythm of giving and receiving, of release and return. It teaches that **abundance doesn't stagnate.** It flows.

What Flows Through You, Grows With You

Abundance is not something you hold onto.
It's something you *move with*.

It's like water.
Try to hoard it — it becomes stagnant.
Try to control it — it slips through your fingers.
But when you let it flow — it nourishes everything it touches…
including you.

The Law of Circulation reminds you:
You are not the source.
You are the channel.

When you give from alignment, you don't lose — you expand.
When you release with trust, you don't lack — you open.

Abundance was never meant to be kept.
It was meant to be *shared, offered, released, received… again and again.*

This is the sacred rhythm.

The Core Teaching

What Is the Law of Circulation?

The Law of Circulation teaches that **abundance is not a fixed amount to be kept — it is a living flow to be honored.**

Everything in nature circulates.

The breath.
The tides.
The seasons.
The giving and receiving of energy, time, money, love.

When something stops moving, it becomes stagnant.
When something flows, it becomes *alive*.

And the same is true with your abundance.

You were not made to grip.
You were made to *flow*.

But when fear takes over — we tighten.
We withhold.
We hoard.
We try to protect what we have by stopping the movement.

But here's the truth:

**Holding too tightly doesn't keep you safe.
It keeps you stuck.**

Circulation is the energy of trust.
When you give from overflow, when you release with intention,
when you allow money, love, ideas, and generosity to move through you —
you become a *magnet* for more.

Not because you're sacrificing.
But because you're in rhythm.

You may be blocking circulation if:

- You give too much and feel resentful or depleted
- You resist spending, even when it's aligned, because it feels unsafe
- You hold back from sharing your gifts, afraid there won't be enough left for you
- You delay decisions, hold grudges, or avoid releasing what's no longer aligned
- You give to get — instead of giving to flow

These are not failures — they are signs that your system has learned to equate release with loss.

But in divine law, **release is how you receive more.**

Circulation does not mean giving everything away.
It means **letting things move freely through you** — with discernment, trust, and generosity.

It means investing in what aligns.
It means receiving without guilt and giving without fear.
It means releasing what you've outgrown — so something new can find you.

When you circulate from truth, you don't diminish what you have.
You multiply it.

This is the sacred rhythm of abundance.
Give. Receive. Release. Return.

Not as a performance.
But as a practice.

The Story or Insight

The Wallet That Wouldn't Open

Imagine someone walking around with a full wallet —
but never using what's inside.

They check it constantly.
They count every bill.
They're afraid to spend, afraid to give, afraid to part with even a little —
because what if nothing comes back?

They don't feel abundant.
They feel scared.
But not because they don't have anything…
because they're afraid to let anything *move*.

So they walk around with a full wallet and an empty life.
They're technically "provided for," but they never feel it.
Why?

Because what they have isn't circulating.
And *abundance without flow becomes fear.*

Maybe you've been there.

You finally get a little ahead — and your first instinct is to **clench**.
You hold on tight.
You stop investing.
You resist spending — even on what you *want*.
You don't give, not because you don't care, but because you feel like you *can't*.

And then things start to stagnate.
Opportunities dry up.

Ideas slow down.
Money doesn't feel joyful — it feels heavy.

You're holding it… but it's not holding you.

Until one day, something softens.
You make one decision — not out of fear, but from trust.

You buy yourself something beautiful, *on purpose*.
You give to someone, not because you "should," but because it *feels right*.
You invest in something that grows you, even if it stretches you.
You release what you were clinging to — time, energy, money — and let it move.

And something shifts.

Not just outside of you.
Inside you.

Because circulation doesn't just change your finances.
It changes your *frequency*.

You realize: you were never the source.
You were the vessel.

And the more freely you let life move through you —
the more fully it flows back.

Living the Law

How to Apply the Law of Circulation in Your Daily Life

Abundance doesn't just grow through asking.
It grows through *movement*.

If you're always receiving but never giving... the flow clogs.
If you're always giving but never receiving... the flow dries up.
But when you **let life move through you — with trust, clarity, and joy — everything expands.**

This isn't about giving everything away.
It's not about being reckless.
It's about learning to **release with faith** — and allow the return to find you.

Let This In: Journal with Compassion

Let these questions gently reveal where your flow has been blocked — and where it's ready to be restored.

- Where in my life am I holding too tightly — to money, time, energy, control?
- Where have I been giving from fear or depletion instead of truth and joy?
- What would it feel like to give, spend, or release from alignment — not guilt or scarcity?

Be honest. You're not being judged.
You're being invited back into the rhythm of trust.

Speak the Truth: Affirmations of Sacred Flow

Say them aloud — or write them down.
These words carry a frequency of *release, expansion, and return.*

I trust the rhythm of circulation.
I release with peace and receive with grace.
What I give from alignment returns multiplied.
There is always more where that came from.
I am not the source — I am the channel.

Embodiment Practice: Let Something Move

Today, practice **circulating energy** from a place of *truth and trust.*

Here are a few simple, powerful ways:

Financial Flow:
Give something from alignment — not pressure.

- Maybe it's a tip, a donation, a gift.
- Maybe it's finally investing in the thing you've been hesitating on, but *know* is right for you.
- Maybe it's choosing to buy something for yourself that reflects self-worth — not survival.

Even a small, intentional act of generosity can crack open a dam inside you.

Ask: *"What would I do with this money if I trusted it would return?"*

Energy + Time:
Let go of what drains you.

- Say no to something you've been holding onto out of guilt.
- Delegate. Delete. Delay — not from avoidance, but clarity.
- Give yourself permission to rest, even if your to-do list is full.

Circulation isn't just about giving to others.
It's about giving energy *back to yourself*, so your flow remains sustainable.

Love + Expression:
Let what's inside you *move outward*.

- Express something you've been holding in — appreciation, forgiveness, encouragement.
- Share a kind word, a message, a truth.
- Open your heart instead of hiding it, even in a small way.

Love is part of circulation, too.
And what you give from a full place will never leave you empty.

The more freely you let life move through you,
the more fully it moves *toward* you.

Circulate something today — not to prove anything.
Just to return to the flow you were born for.

Final Whisper

You were never meant to hold it all.
You were meant to let it move through you.
The time.
The love.
The money.
The beauty.
The breath.

What you give from trust does not leave you empty.
It leaves you open.

You don't have to clench to stay safe.
You don't have to grip to stay abundant.
You don't have to hoard what you were made to share.

So give when it feels true.
Release when it's time.
Say yes to flow.

You are not the dam.
You are the river.

And the current you allow will always carry you home.

Chapter Ten

The Law of Expansion
You Are Safe to Have More

This one is huge — it's where the reader confronts the *edges of their abundance*. The parts of them that still fear more success, more money, more love, more visibility… and gently learns to open instead of shrink.

You Are Safe to Have More

You were never meant to stay small.
You were meant to grow, stretch, rise, and expand —
not just spiritually, but practically.

More money.
More joy.
More impact.
More love.
More ease.
Not because more makes you worthy —
but because *you were always worthy of more.*

The Law of Expansion reminds you:
You don't receive more by grasping…
You receive more by *allowing yourself to hold it.*

And the truth is:
Most people aren't blocked by their limits —
they're blocked by their *threshold*.

They only allow in what they feel safe to keep.

But today, that changes.

You're not here to shrink.

You're here to expand — without guilt, without fear, without apology.

The Core Teaching

What Is the Law of Expansion?

The Law of Expansion teaches this simple truth:

You only receive what you feel safe to have.

Not what you *desire*.
Not what you *pray for*.
What you feel **safe**, **ready**, and **worthy** enough to hold.

Most people think they're blocked because they don't have enough.
But often… they're blocked because they don't feel safe with *more*.

You ask for more money —
but deep down, fear how it would change your relationships.
You long for more love —
but worry that more intimacy means more risk.
You want your business to grow —
but you're afraid of being seen, judged, or overwhelmed.

So without realizing it, you shrink.
You say no to opportunities.
You sabotage the moment it starts working.
You undercharge. You stay quiet.
You delay the leap. You downplay the dream.

Not because you don't want more —
but because you haven't yet decided it's safe to *have* more.

This is your *expansion threshold*.
The invisible line that says: *"This is how much I'm allowed to have before it becomes too much."*

That line is not set by the Universe.
It was created by fear.
By old beliefs.
By survival.
By stories that told you…

- "You can't have it all."

- "If you have more, someone else will have less."

- "People won't like the new version of you."

- "You'll be judged if you shine."

- "You won't be able to handle it."

- "It's safer to stay where you are."

But the truth is:
You are allowed to stretch without snapping.
You are allowed to grow without guilt.
You are allowed to have more… and *still be loved, safe, grounded, and good.*

Expansion is not always easy.
It brings things up.
Old fears, old identities, old patterns.

But expansion is also **natural**.
You were made to grow.
To receive more. To hold more. To become more.

The question is no longer, *"Can I have more?"*
The question is:
"Can I feel safe letting it in?"

And the answer… can become yes.

The Story or Insight

The Moment It Got "Too Good"

Maybe you know the feeling.

Things are going *better* than usual.
You finally get ahead.
Money flows in.
You feel clear, aligned, grounded.
The work is working. The love feels safe. The opportunities are opening.

And then… something inside you pulls back.

You suddenly get tired.
You pick a fight.
You stop showing up.
You sabotage the project.
You make a decision you know isn't aligned — but feels familiar.

Why?
Because some part of you decided:
"This is too good. I don't know how to hold this."

We all have a threshold.
A hidden thermostat for how much good we're used to.
And when life starts rising above that setting — we subconsciously cool it back down.

Not because we're broken —
but because our nervous system is still wired for "just enough."

Not overflow. Not ease. Not thriving.

But expansion isn't about pushing further.
It's about gently raising the setting.
Letting yourself sit in the *new normal* of more — and stay there.

- More ease, without panic.

- More money, without guilt.

- More joy, without sabotage.

- More visibility, without fear of being too much.

It's not always comfortable — but it's powerful.

Because the moment you choose to stay open…
the threshold begins to dissolve.

You breathe deeper.
You stop apologizing.
You start letting it be this good —
without shrinking to make others comfortable
or sabotaging to stay "realistic."

Expansion doesn't require you to do more.
It asks you to *hold* more.
With peace.
With softness.
With grace.

That's when the abundance stops peaking and crashing —
and starts *staying*.

Living the Law

How to Apply the Law of Expansion in Your Daily Life

Most people don't fear lack —
they fear *what will happen if they actually get what they want.*

Because more brings up your edge.

More visibility can bring fear of judgment.
More money can bring guilt, or pressure to be perfect.
More love can bring fear of loss or abandonment.
More success can trigger unworthiness.

So the question is not, *"Am I ready for more?"*
It's, *"Can I feel safe while holding more?"*

This law teaches you to gently increase your capacity.
To stay open even when your body wants to shrink.
To breathe through the discomfort of goodness — and let it stay.

Let This In: Journal with Compassion

These questions help you see where your expansion has been hitting its edge — and how you can soften past it.

- What "level" of abundance, joy, love, or money feels normal to me? What feels "too much"?

- What do I fear might happen if I suddenly receive more of what I've been asking for?

- Where do I tend to pull back, sabotage, or shut down when things start working?

Your threshold isn't your fault — it's your starting place.
Now you get to raise it — gently, honestly, and with love.

Speak the Truth: Affirmations of Expansion

Let these affirmations create a new baseline inside you — one where more is safe, grounded, and normal.

I am safe to expand.
I am safe to have more.
I am safe to hold success, love, money, peace — without fear.
I no longer sabotage what I once prayed for.
I let the goodness stay.

Embodiment Practice: Let It Be "Too Good"

Today, practice *holding more* — not by doing more, but by *not shrinking* when good things arrive.

Here are a few ways this might look in your life:

When you receive more money than usual:
Don't immediately balance it out by overspending or downplaying it.
Pause. Let it land.
Say: *"It's safe to hold this. I'm allowed to keep it."*

Let yourself feel peace, not panic.

When someone compliments, celebrates, or uplifts you:
Don't deflect. Don't brush it off.
Say: *"Thank you. I'm letting that in."*
Let your nervous system *learn* that being seen is safe.

When things are flowing:
If you notice the urge to create drama, fix something, or stir the pot — pause.
You don't have to earn your goodness.
You don't have to make it harder to make it feel real.

Let ease be enough.
Let the flow be the proof.

Extra Practice:
Do something today that reflects the level of life you're stepping into — even if it stretches you.

- Upgrade something small (your environment, your schedule, your self-talk)

- Make a bold choice that reflects the *expanded* version of you

- Or simply *stay present* in a moment of goodness without shrinking, distracting, or rushing

---

Expansion is a nervous system experience.
And the more often you breathe through the edge —
the more natural abundance begins to feel.

Let it stretch you.
And let it stay.

Final Whisper

Whether you've never had enough…
or never felt safe enough to hold what you had…
this is where the story changes.

More was never the enemy.
You were simply learning how to receive it
without fear.
Without shrinking.
Without believing it would cost you your peace.

You are strong enough to hold the life you've been asking for.
You are safe enough to stay open when the good arrives.
You are worthy enough to let it be this beautiful.

Expansion isn't a race.
It's a softening.
A remembering.

A remembering that you are not too much —
and neither is the dream.

So let it come.
Let it stretch you.
Let it rise in your hands.

Let more be your new normal.
And let it stay.

Chapter Eleven

The Law of Devotion

Let Your Life Become the Practice

This chapter is the *sacred sealing* of the teachings —
It's no longer just about what you believe, receive, or do.
It's about how you *live* — moment by moment, breath by breath, as an offering.

You don't just attract abundance.
You become someone who *embodies it* — *daily, deeply, devotionally.*

Let Your Life Become the Practice

Abundance isn't just a moment.
It's a rhythm.
A relationship.
A way of being.

You don't have to keep starting over.
You don't have to wait until you feel ready again.
You just have to keep returning — with devotion.

The Law of Devotion says:
You become what you stay faithful to.
Not once. Not perfectly.
But over time, with love, with breath, with practice.

Devotion is how you turn insight into embodiment.
How you walk when the feelings fade.
How you stay rooted in truth —
not because it's easy, but because it's yours.

This is no longer about the tools.
It's about who you are when no one's watching.
It's about the way you speak to yourself, the way you breathe through resistance,
the way you keep your heart open when it would be easier to shut down.

Devotion is not discipline.
It's love in motion.

And that's what keeps the abundance flowing.

The Core Teaching

What Is the Law of Devotion?

The Law of Devotion teaches us that:

Your life becomes what you return to.

Not what you visit once in a while.
Not what you believe when it's easy.
Not what you write in your journal and then forget.

Your life reflects your devotion.

Devotion isn't about perfection.
It's not a set of rules or routines.
It's not about being high-vibe 24/7.

It's about choosing your truth again and again,
even when you're tired.
Even when fear is louder.
Even when no one else sees it but you.

Devotion means you keep showing up —
not because you're chasing the result,
but because this path *matters to you*.

You've learned the Laws.
You've felt the shift.
You've seen what's possible.

Now the question is:
Will you stay with it when the results aren't instant?
Will you stay with it when life gets loud again?
Will you walk this path when no one is clapping?

That's devotion.

The choice to keep watering what you planted —
to keep practicing what you know is true —
to keep becoming the person you were born to be,
even when your ego wants a shortcut.

Devotion is how you graduate from dabbling… to embodying.
From spiritual "interest" to sacred *integration*.

It's the way you turn truth into transformation.

And the good news?

You don't need to do it perfectly.
You don't need to do it all at once.
You just need to keep coming back — to the breath, the rhythm, the truth.

One honest return at a time.

And here's what devotion makes possible:

When you stay with the truth — even quietly, even imperfectly —
your life begins to bloom in ways you couldn't have imagined.

You begin to shine without forcing it.
You begin to attract without chasing.
You begin to live in a way that feels whole, holy, and *fully yours*.

This path will change you —
not with pressure, but with power.
Not overnight, but over time.
And if you stay with it…

You will become more free, more fulfilled, and more radiant than you ever thought possible.

Because abundance doesn't just visit the devoted.
It lives with them.

The Story or Insight

The One Who Came Back

Maybe it wasn't every day.
Maybe they missed weeks.
Maybe they had seasons of doubt.
Maybe they fell back into fear, into hustle, into forgetting.

But they always returned.

They came back to their breath.
To their truth.
To their vision.
To the path that felt like home.

And that's what made the difference.
Not that they were perfect —
but that they were *devoted.*

You don't need to always get it right.
You don't need to always feel clear, high-vibe, or fearless.
But what will change your life is this:

You come back.
You forgive yourself.
You remember the truth.
You return to your alignment — *on an ordinary Tuesday afternoon,* not just at rock bottom.

And over time, the return becomes the rhythm.
The rhythm becomes your baseline.
And your baseline becomes your life.

Devotion doesn't mean you never wobble.
It means you don't wander forever.

You stop leaving yourself for too long.
You stop betraying your knowing.
You start noticing when you've slipped — and you reach for your anchor.

That's how you build a life you can trust.
That's how peace becomes normal.
That's how wealth becomes sustainable.
That's how alignment becomes your atmosphere —
not because you mastered the moment…
but because you *stayed with it*.

And over time…

Things begin to flow where they used to feel stuck.
Money arrives more often — and stays longer.
You feel calm even in the unknown.
You speak to yourself like someone who is loved.
You walk into rooms differently.
You expect goodness, not just hope for it.
And you stop chasing what you used to think you had to earn —
because now, it comes to you.

Your life doesn't just change.
It becomes a mirror of who you truly are.

Devotion made you into someone who doesn't just believe in abundance —
but lives inside it.

And that is what changes everything.

Living the Law

How to Apply the Law of Devotion in Your Daily Life

This is the law that holds all the others.
Not because it demands perfection — but because it invites *return*.

You won't always feel aligned.
You won't always get it "right."
But that's not what devotion is about.

Devotion is how you walk —
not just when the path is clear,
but when it's cloudy, quiet, or slow.

It's how you keep your life open to abundance
even when fear tries to close it down.

Let This In: Journal with Compassion

Use these questions to come back to yourself — gently, honestly, lovingly.

- What does devotion look like for me right now — in a way that feels sustainable and soul-honoring?

- Where do I tend to give up or disappear when I feel off-track?

- What am I ready to return to — without shame, without guilt, just because I love who I'm becoming?

Let this be a homecoming.
You're not starting over — you're starting *from truth*.

Speak the Truth: Affirmations of Sacred Return

Say these when you're clear. Say them when you're lost.
Say them when you need to remember who you are.

I return to my truth — again and again.
My alignment is not fragile. It's faithful.
I don't have to be perfect — I just have to come back.
My devotion builds a life I can trust.
I stay with what matters to me.

Embodiment Practice: Build Your Rhythm

Choose one simple, sacred rhythm that you can return to — daily, weekly, gently.

It could be:

- **A morning devotion practice:** lighting a candle, reading one line from this book, saying one affirmation with your hand on your heart

- **A weekly check-in:** asking, "Where am I aligned? Where do I want to return?" and letting that guide your next week

- **A ritual when you feel off:** something you do *not to fix*, but to *recenter* — like a walk, a prayer, a breath, a journal line

- **A promise to yourself:** to return without punishment, without pressure, without performing — just because this path is *yours*

Devotion doesn't ask you to do more.
It asks you to love what you return to.

Choose one thing. Let it be light. Let it be real.
And let it be the rhythm that keeps your life in flow.

Final Whisper

You don't have to be perfect.
You don't have to be unshakable.
You don't have to be high-vibe every moment of your life.

You just have to stay close to your truth.

You just have to keep returning —
to the vision,
to the rhythm,
to the quiet knowing that lives inside you.

Devotion isn't a performance.
It's presence.

And it's the most powerful choice you can make.

Because the longer you stay with this path —
the clearer it becomes.

The more you walk in alignment —
the more abundance rises to meet your steps.

And what once felt far away becomes your new atmosphere.

This isn't just what you do.
It's who you are now.

So stay with it.
Even when it's quiet.
Even when it's hard.
Even when no one sees it but you.

Because this devotion —
this quiet, steady, sacred returning —
is what makes your life overflow.

Chapter 12

The Law Beyond the Law
Live as the Proof

This is the final breath, the golden seal, the quiet fire that says:
You're no longer seeking. You're walking proof.

Live as the Proof

This is the moment you stop trying to "get it right."
And start *being who you truly are.*

You're not just here to understand abundance.
You're here to *embody it.*

Not to quote it.
Not to perform it.
But to become the living, breathing evidence
that alignment creates overflow.
That peace can be powerful.
That wealth can be sacred.
That devotion works.

This is the law beyond the law —
the moment when you stop practicing the path
and *become the path.*

You don't have to explain it.
You don't have to justify it.
You just have to live it —
in your posture, your choices, your energy, your presence.

Because now…
you are the proof.

The Core Teaching

What Is the Law Beyond the Law?

The Law Beyond the Law is the moment the path becomes your posture.

It's no longer about choosing the truth again and again —
because now, the truth is *who you are*.

You're not just aligning when things get hard.
You're aligned because it's your natural state.
You've practiced. You've walked. You've returned.
And now — you *radiate*.

This law is not about returning to alignment.
It's about *living from alignment*.
It's not about remembering who you are.
It's about *being it — unapologetically, consistently, silently powerful.*

You no longer need to prove it.
You no longer need to push for it.
You simply *embody it* —
in the way you speak, in the way you choose, in the way you show up without effort.

You're not performing for approval.
You're not trying to convince the world.
You're just living so fully in your truth
that your life becomes undeniable evidence.

There's a difference between trying to prove something
and *being the proof*.

One drains you.
The other **elevates** everything around you.

You are no longer chasing abundance.
You are holding it.
You are no longer waiting for your life to reflect your worth —
you are building a life that *proves it*.

Your presence becomes your message.
Your peace becomes your power.
Your embodiment becomes your magnet.

People feel it before you say a word.
Doors open before you ask.
Money flows not because you force it — but because you've *become* a vessel it trusts.

You don't have to follow the rules anymore.
You *are* the rhythm now.
You're not practicing the Law.
You're *living as the Law in motion*.

You are the proof.
Not because you're perfect.
But because you are true.

And truth is magnetic.

The Story or Insight

This Is What It Looks Like Now

They used to second-guess everything.
Their worth.
Their timing.
Their voice.
Their enoughness.

They used to shrink before they spoke.
They used to wait for permission.
They used to try to prove they deserved more.

But something shifted.

Not all at once.
Not overnight.
But deeply.

It wasn't a breakthrough.
It was a becoming.

Now…

They check their bank account — and see overflow, not survival.
They rest — and don't spiral with guilt.
They walk into the room — and don't shrink to fit.
They receive compliments — and let them land.
They ask for what they want — and don't apologize for needing it.

Not because they became perfect.
But because they *stopped arguing with who they are.*

They no longer have to say "I'm abundant."
They just *are.*

In the way they speak.
In the way they create.
In the way they move through money with clarity and joy.
In the way they hold wealth without fear.
In the way they breathe.

Their alignment is visible.
Their worth is *felt*.
Their energy does the speaking now.

Maybe you don't feel that every day yet.
Maybe you're still stretching into it.
But here's the truth:

Every time you choose to walk in alignment —
even quietly, even invisibly —
you become the proof.

You become the one who no longer waits for external validation because your *existence* is already evidence.

Evidence that peace is magnetic.
Evidence that alignment attracts.
Evidence that you can create a life
that's whole, holy, wealthy, and real.

You don't need to try harder.
You just need to *be the one who lives it.*

Living the Law

How to Apply the Law Beyond the Law in Your Daily Life

This isn't about tools anymore.
It's about identity.

You don't need to fix, prove, or chase.
You just need to live like someone who knows the truth —
because you do.

You've remembered who you are.
Now let your life reflect it.

Let This In: Journal with Clarity

You've walked the path.
You've shifted your inner world.
Now it's time to acknowledge what's already becoming real.

Use these questions to honor the evidence — and anchor it deeper.

- What has changed in how I think, feel, speak, or move since I began this journey?

- How do I relate to money, rest, asking, trusting, or receiving — *now* versus before?

- What new opportunities, ideas, or forms of abundance have started to appear in my life?

- What am I most proud of in the way I've chosen to live this path?

- What proof is already showing up — that I am the embodiment of these laws?

Let this be your reflection.
Let it be your recognition.
Let it be the moment you say:

"This is working.
I am walking it.
And my life is beginning to show it."

Speak the Truth: Identity Affirmations

Say them from your core.
Say them as a declaration — not a wish.

I am the embodiment of abundance.
My life is a reflection of my alignment.
I don't have to chase what I carry.
I am the evidence that wealth can be sacred.
I live as the proof — quietly, powerfully, freely.

Embodiment Practice: Walk Like It's Already True

You don't need a ritual to become.
You already are.

Now — let your choices reflect that truth.

Just one action today.

Taken calmly, clearly, confidently.

- Raise your prices.
- Stop apologizing for resting.
- Invest in something that reflects your worth.
- Say no to what no longer matches your frequency.

- Walk into that room, that call, that creation —
  and let your energy speak *for you*.

Let today be a mirror of who you've become.
Not for performance.
But because it's true.

You don't need permission.
You *are* the law now.

Final Whisper

You've walked the path.
Not perfectly — but honestly.
Not all at once — but with presence.

You've remembered who you are.
You've felt what alignment can unlock.
You've tasted what it means to live in the rhythm of abundance.

And now...

You don't need to say another affirmation.
You don't need to wait for another sign.
You don't need to reach for what you already carry.

You are the proof.

Not because you've mastered the moment —
but because you've chosen to stay close to your truth.

You are the one who creates from peace.
Who receives without guilt.
Who circulates with joy.
Who lives with intention.
Who lets it be *this good* — and lets it stay.

You don't just follow the laws now.
You *are the law in motion.*

And when you live that way —
everything begins to rise to meet you.

So go live it.
Not to convince.
Not to perform.
But because your life is already the evidence.
Because truth doesn't have to prove itself.

It just has to be lived.
And that's what you're doing now.

Wealth in Motion: How the 12 Laws Turn Abundance into Financial Reality

Why Money Matters

Money is not separate from your spiritual journey.
It is not a lesser desire.
It is not shallow, selfish, or shameful.

Money is a mirror.
A reflection of how safe, worthy, and aligned you feel to receive.

It reveals what you believe about support.
It reflects how fully you've allowed yourself to be seen, valued, and held.
It asks:
"Are you ready to receive in form what you've already claimed in truth?"

You were not meant to struggle endlessly with money.
You were not meant to just "make it work."
You were not born to survive.

You were born to flow.
To circulate.
To expand.
To become a vessel through which wealth blesses not only your life — but others.

This is not about loving money more than peace.
It's about realizing that **money can be a vessel for peace.**
That wealth can be sacred.
That overflow can be a form of devotion.

Money is not a test.
It is not a distraction.
It is an *invitation* —
to let abundance become real.

Not just in your vision board.
But in your bank account.
Your income.
Your lifestyle.
Your legacy.

You've walked the path.
You've shifted the inner world.
Now let's show you how the outer world — including money —
begins to move in response.

This is wealth in motion.
This is how it begins to *arrive*.

How the 12 Laws Shape Your Financial Life

The 12 Laws weren't just preparing you for peace.
They were preparing you for *prosperity*.

Here's how each one transforms your relationship with money:

1. The Law of Divine Inheritance

"You don't have to earn abundance. You were born with it."

You stop believing money is for "other people."
You remember you were born to receive — not just enough, but *more than enough*.

2. The Law of Belief

"You don't manifest what you want — you manifest what you expect."

You uncover the unconscious beliefs that kept money at arm's length —
and you begin to rewrite what you expect to earn, keep, and grow.

3. The Law of Worthiness

"You don't receive more because you're perfect — you receive more because you believe you're allowed to."

You stop undercharging, shrinking, and apologizing.
You let yourself be paid well — without guilt or hesitation.

4. The Law of Alignment

"Abundance flows where you flow."

You stop forcing income through misaligned paths.
You choose work that feels energizing — and let money follow your truth.

---

5. The Law of Timing

"You are not late. You are not behind. You are inside a divine unfolding."

You stop panicking when the results aren't instant.
You begin to trust the pacing — and hold your vision without rushing.

---

6. The Law of Embodiment

"You don't receive when you become worthy — you receive when you become ready."

You shift your posture, your boundaries, and your energy.
You start treating yourself like someone who is already supported — and money begins to respond.

---

7. The Law of Inspired Action

"Aligned action opens aligned results."

You take bold, clear steps — from a place of inner certainty.
And income begins to *move toward you*.

8. The Law of Receiving

"You're not blocked from abundance — you're just not used to letting it in."

You stop sabotaging when money arrives.
You stop flinching when ease enters.
You start letting it *stay*.

---

9. The Law of Circulation

"What you give and how you spend reveals what you believe."

You give from sufficiency, not sacrifice.
You spend from alignment, not anxiety.
And your relationship with money becomes one of sacred flow.

---

10. The Law of Expansion

"More is not a threat — it's your new normal."

You stop capping your income at what's "comfortable."
You stretch into overflow — and allow yourself to *hold it*.

---

11. The Law of Devotion

"What you stay faithful to… multiplies."

You don't give up on the vision.
You keep showing up — and wealth becomes not just possible…
but *sustainable*.

12. The Law Beyond the Law

"You are the proof."

You no longer talk about abundance — you *embody it*.
You no longer try to attract money — your life naturally holds and multiplies it.
You live in overflow. Quietly. Powerfully. Freely.

PART ONE: You Want to Start Something New

1. Laying the Ground

Before you launch — you align.

You don't need the perfect idea.
You don't need all the answers.
You don't need a 10-step business plan before you begin.

You need a foundation rooted in clarity, alignment, and willingness to move.

That's what changes everything.

Starting something new isn't about chasing trends or jumping at the first opportunity that promises quick money.
It's about building something that feels **true** — and letting your wealth grow from that truth.

Step 1: Get Clear on What *You* Actually Want

Don't start with what's popular.
Start with what feels like *you*.

Ask yourself:

- What kind of work would I love to wake up to?
- What kind of energy do I want to live inside every day?
- Do I want freedom? Simplicity? Expression? Purpose? Connection?

You don't need to know the exact form yet.
But you do need to know the *feeling* you're building toward.

That's what allows the right ideas to find you.

Step 2: Explore the Ideas That Feel Alive

Once the feeling is clear — start playing.

You can explore ideas like:

- What do people naturally come to me for?
- What would I love to learn, teach, or create — even if no one paid me at first?
- If I could create anything and know it would work, what would I try?

This is where you let **inspiration rise** without judgment.
No filtering yet. Just curiosity and openness.

Step 3: Begin the Aligned Research (for real)

This is where inspiration becomes direction.

If you're serious about creating a new source of income — one that feels aligned and sustainable — this is where your **devotion meets structure.**

Start by choosing **one direction** that feels alive — not perfect, just *promising.*

Then, make the commitment to begin a focused research phase.
Not a scroll, not a mood board — but actual discovery, learning, *building understanding.*

Devote at least 3–5 days (or more) to this early research stage:

- Explore people doing something similar
- Watch their offers, platforms, content, and pricing
- Note what resonates — and what doesn't
- Learn about the business models behind the idea
- Write down what you'd need to learn, upgrade, or gather to move forward

This is not pressure.
This is permission to go deeper.

Don't try to build the whole thing in a weekend.
But do give your vision the respect of **real investigation.**

Let yourself begin gathering tools, inspiration, ideas.
Even if it's messy at first — *it's motion.*
It's how momentum is born.

A Sacred Reminder Before You Move Forward

You will hear a lot of people say:
"You *have* to make money online."
"You *should* start a business."
"You *must* choose something scalable."

But here's the truth:

If you build something that feels misaligned — even if it's profitable —
you won't just struggle to succeed...
you'll build a life you resent.

If every hour you spend on your business feels heavy...
If every task drains your energy or triggers dread...
Then no amount of income will feel like abundance.

Because if you hate what you're doing every day —

you're not building wealth.
You're building a life you want to escape from.

So ask yourself honestly:

- Could I enjoy the process of this, not just the outcome?
- Would I still want to do this even if it took time to grow?
- Can I see this being part of my life — not just my strategy?

If the answer is no — don't force it.
You are allowed to create something that feels light, meaningful, and *true to your rhythm.*

That's where real wealth begins.

2. Creating Movement

From Idea to Initial Action

Ideas are beautiful.
But wealth doesn't come from ideas.
It comes from **embodied direction.**

This is the part most people skip.
Not because they're lazy — but because it's *heavy* to start walking a new road.
Because staying where you are — even if it's unfulfilling — is *familiar.*
You know how it feels. You know what to expect.
You don't have to stretch, risk, or reach for more.

It's not fear alone that keeps people stuck.
It's the comfort of what they've survived.

And to choose something new?
That takes energy.
That takes vision.
That takes *faith* — the kind that believes in a reality you haven't lived yet.

Faith and fear both require belief in the unseen.
One builds your future. The other keeps you circling the past.
You choose.

There is no perfect moment to begin.
There is only the moment you *stop waiting for proof,*
and start becoming it.

Because here's the truth:

**The devil doesn't have to chase you
if he can convince you to stop walking.**

But you — you are *not done moving*.
You are not too late.
You are not too tired to rise.

In ten years, you will either be deeply grateful you began…
or still wondering if it's too late.

This is the moment that shifts the timeline.
This is wealth in motion.

Step 1: Choose a Direction — Not Forever, Just for Now

You don't have to commit to this path for life.
But you do need to commit long enough to see what it could become.

Choose one idea.
Just one.

And name it:

- I'm starting a coaching offer
- I'm offering handmade products
- I'm testing a healing service
- I'm starting a content-based project (podcast, channel, blog, etc.)
- I'm creating a digital product, teaching, or membership

Write it down. Speak it out loud.
Even if it's a whisper.
This is how something new begins.

Step 2: Build the Simplest First Offer or Format

Forget the 10-step funnel.
Forget the fancy branding.
Right now, you're proving that it can *move*.

Build a version of your offer in its **simplest, most honest form**:

- A 1:1 session you can offer
- A simple product listing
- A PayPal link and a post
- A written outline of a service you can test
- A short piece of content that starts your presence

You're not building the empire.
You're **building the muscle.**

Money doesn't come when you're ready.
It comes when you're *in motion*.

Step 3: Share It — Imperfectly and Now

This is where energy starts circulating.
Even if you don't feel "ready."
Even if you're scared.
Even if 10 people see it instead of 10,000.

- Share it with someone you trust
- Post about it (soft or bold — your style)
- Invite 1 person to try it
- Create a sample, or do a quiet beta round

- Let people know *you're open*

It's not about going viral.
It's about showing the Universe: *I'm not hiding anymore.*

This part might feel awkward.
It might feel small.
But it's the most sacred step of all:

You are no longer dreaming about wealth.
You are *welcoming* it — through action.

3. Let Yourself Learn

You're Building Something Real — Not Rushing a Miracle

Starting something new is courageous.
But *staying with it long enough to learn* — that's how you build something lasting.

You're not just launching a project.
You're building *skills*, *systems*, and *self-trust*.
And that takes time.

So here's the permission most people never hear:

You don't have to get it all right from the beginning.
But you do need to be willing to *learn as you go*.

Step 1: Learn From Doing

The most valuable lessons don't come from reading about them — they come from *trying, failing, adjusting, and trying again*.

You might:

- Offer something and get little response — so you refine it

- Price something too low or too high — and adjust from experience

- Realize you love part of what you created — and pivot your model

- Get feedback that helps you sharpen your message or your process

This is not failure.
This is how you build real, lived wisdom.
Let yourself experiment.

Step 2: Learn From Others

There is no prize for doing everything alone.

Yes, your path is unique —
but someone else has walked a version of it *before you*.

Find people who reflect what's possible — and learn from them.

That might look like:

- Taking a course from someone whose energy and values resonate

- Reading or listening to content that teaches what you're building

- Hiring a coach or mentor — even for a short season

- Joining a small circle, mastermind, or community where you can be supported

You don't need to take every course.
You don't need to buy someone else's blueprint.
But you *do* need to **take learning seriously** — the way someone does when they're building something that matters.

Step 3: Give Yourself Time to Grow

No one becomes a master by accident.
No one builds long-term wealth by skipping the season of learning.

You are still building your roots.
Let this part take time.

Don't compare your first chapter to someone's tenth.
Don't shame yourself for needing help.
Don't rush to "arrive" before you've practiced how to stand.

You are learning.
You are growing.
And *this* — this is what makes your wealth sustainable.

Step 4: Let It Take Time — And That's Okay

Not succeeding right away doesn't mean you're failing.
It doesn't mean you're doing it wrong.
It doesn't mean abundance isn't meant for you.

It just means… you're in the process.

You are not late.
You are not behind.
You are not being punished.
You are *becoming* — and becoming takes time.

Don't rush to scale before you've stabilized.
Don't pressure yourself to earn five figures in your first month.
Don't confuse someone else's highlight reel with your sacred beginning.

This is your path.
And it is unfolding in divine rhythm.

The Laws are always working — even when the results take time to show.
If you keep aligning, acting, and opening… *you will not miss what's meant for you.*

Stay with it.
Keep walking.
Let your devotion outrun your doubt.

Because wealth that lasts is never built in a weekend.
It's built in rhythm.
In refinement.
In trust.

4. Being Seen & Receiving

Letting the Flow Actually Reach You

You've done the hardest part — you've moved.
You've started.
You've created.
You've made yourself available for something new.

Now comes the next threshold:

Can you let yourself be seen?
Can you let yourself be paid?
Can you let it be real — and not run when it arrives?

This is where so many beautiful souls shrink.
Not because they're not ready — but because they still believe they have to *earn the right to receive.*

But here's the truth:

You don't have to be more perfect to be more visible.
You don't have to be more experienced to be well-paid.
You don't have to prove anything before you're allowed to begin.

You are allowed to let people see what you're building.
You are allowed to ask for compensation that honors your energy.
You are allowed to *be open.*

Step 1: Let People Know You're Available

This part isn't about marketing strategy.
It's about *energetic availability.*

Letting people know:

- What you're offering

- Who it's for
- How to access or experience it

Share it with:

- A friend or trusted circle
- A story, post, or video
- A quiet announcement to people who've asked about your gifts
- Your existing community, no matter how small

It doesn't have to be polished.
But it *does* have to be visible.

Energy needs an invitation to circulate.

Step 2: Price with Peace — Not Panic

You don't have to undercharge to be "fair."
You don't have to be the cheapest to be chosen.
You don't have to match what others charge to be legitimate.

Ask:

- What price honors my time, energy, and experience — even if it's early?
- What amount would feel like a true exchange — not depletion?
- Can I let money land in my hands without apology?

Money is not a reward. It's a reflection.
Let it reflect your worth — not your doubt.

Step 3: Let It Land

When someone buys, supports, invests, or pays:

- Receive it *consciously*
- Breathe
- Smile
- Let your nervous system *register* that it's safe to be paid
- Say thank you without shrinking, deflecting, or explaining

This is how you train your body to hold more.
This is how you teach the Universe: *"I'm ready now."*

Let it be simple. Let it be sacred.
You are not taking — you are circulating.

This is wealth… *meeting you where you finally stood still long enough to receive it.*

5. Letting It Grow

Stay Long Enough to Witness the Bloom

You don't have to build fast.
You just have to stay with it long enough to watch it work.

This is the part most people abandon — not because they weren't capable, but because they got impatient.
Because the results didn't come fast enough.
Because they didn't *feel* like it was working.

But here's what the Laws will always tell you:

Everything multiplies under devotion.
Everything blooms in its own season.

Step 1: Commit to Consistency — Not Perfection

You don't have to be visible every day.
You don't have to create content constantly.
You don't have to launch endlessly.

But you *do* have to show up — with rhythm, not urgency.

That might look like:

- Sending one honest message a week
- Taking one aligned action every day
- Improving one piece of your offer each month
- Taking a small break *and returning*
- Celebrating every payment, every message, every shift — as sacred

This is how businesses grow.
This is how money becomes movement.

Not through hype.
But through harmony.

Step 2: Keep Refining, Not Reinventing

You don't need a new idea every week.
You need to keep returning to the one that's true — and deepen your craft inside it.

That might mean:

- Raising your price after you've served with love
- Adding clarity to your message or offer
- Evolving your brand as you evolve
- Learning new tools or skills that help you serve better
- Asking for feedback — not from fear, but from devotion to the work

The wealth comes in waves —
but the foundation is built in stillness, in repetition, in return.

Step 3: Let the Laws Keep Holding You

When it feels slow, return to Belief.
When fear creeps in, return to Worthiness.
When doubt knocks, return to Devotion.

You already have the tools.
You've already learned the way.

You are no longer chasing success —
You are building the capacity to hold it.

And you're doing it now. Quietly. Powerfully. Faithfully.

PART TWO: You Want to Rise Where You Already Are

1. Clarify What You Actually Want

Sometimes we say we want "more" — but we haven't named what that actually means.

And when your vision is vague, your results will be too.

Before you can rise, you have to define what *rising* looks like for you.

So start here:

Ask Yourself With Total Honesty:

- Do I want a higher income — and if so, how much more?
- Do I want a promotion, a raise, a leadership role?
- Do I want more freedom or flexibility within my role?
- Do I want a different position — either inside or outside this company?
- Do I want to feel more expressed, respected, or aligned?

You don't need to have the full plan yet.
But you *do* need to tell the truth.

This is where *momentum begins* — with a vision you're willing to own.

Write a Clear Statement of Desire:

Not to manifest it perfectly — but to **activate clarity.**

Examples:

- "I want to move into a role that pays me $X/month and honors my creative strengths."
- "I want to ask for a raise of 20% based on the value I bring."
- "I want to work with clients who energize me, not deplete me."
- "I want to shift into a team, company, or contract that reflects who I've become."

Say it clearly.
Write it down.
Breathe it in.

You can't rise if you're still pretending you're fine where you are.

2. Clean the Energy

You Can't Rise in a Space You Secretly Resent

It's hard to rise in a job, business, or structure that you secretly resent — but still rely on.
It creates friction. Self-protection. Emotional shutdown.
You feel tired, stuck, or even invisible.

But the energy you bring to your current reality is the same energy that determines what's possible *next*.

If you curse the space you're in, you stay anchored to it.
If you bring clarity, ownership, and presence — you create an energetic opening.

This is not about tolerating what isn't aligned.
It's about transforming how you show up while you *build your next level*.

Step 1: Shift from Resentment to Authority

Instead of "I hate this job," ask:

- *What am I still here to learn, refine, or embody?*
- *Where am I outsourcing my power — and how can I call it back?*
- *What would it look like to bring more excellence, presence, or integrity — for me, not them?*

You're not doing it for your boss.
You're doing it to align with the level of energy you want to live in next.

If you want to lead... start leading here.
If you want to be trusted with more... steward what's already in your hands.

Step 2: Notice What You're Still Tolerating

What you tolerate *teaches the world how to treat you* — including clients, coworkers, and employers.

Ask yourself:

- What patterns do I keep agreeing to, even though they drain me?
- Where do I say yes when I mean no?
- Where have I been underpaid, undervalued, or unexpressed — but afraid to disrupt it?

You're not here to tolerate your way into a better life.
You're here to **realign.**

Even small energetic upgrades — like setting a boundary, speaking a truth, or cleaning up your calendar — change your field.

Step 3: Reclaim Your Vision From the Inside

Your current environment doesn't define your next level — your **energy inside it does.**

When you show up with intention, not resentment...
The entire field begins to shift.

Sometimes the opportunity evolves.
Sometimes *you* evolve out of it.

But either way — you become magnetic to the next version of wealth, work, and self-expression.

This is not pretending.
This is *preparing*.

3. Ask & Act From Power

You Are Not Waiting to Be Chosen — You Are Choosing Yourself

Most people don't stay small because they're not capable —
They stay small because they're waiting.

Waiting to be noticed.
Waiting to be praised.
Waiting for someone else to say, *"You deserve more."*

But here's the truth:

No one can raise your life if you won't raise your hand.

It's not entitled to ask for a raise.
It's not dramatic to shift roles.
It's not arrogant to pursue more ease, more pay, more purpose.

It's alignment.
It's self-leadership.
It's **financial sovereignty** in action.

Step 1: Ask For What You Know You Deserve

This doesn't mean demanding more with tension.
It means requesting more from *alignment*.

Ask yourself:

- Where am I being underpaid — and what do I now know I'm worthy of?

- Where can I ask for a raise, a title shift, or a role that reflects my growth?

- Where can I communicate my vision clearly — not with desperation, but with clarity?

When you ask, remember:

- You don't need to justify your value — you need to *stand in it*
- You don't need to apologize for evolving — you need to *embody it*
- You don't need permission — you need *a voice that reflects the version of you who's already there*

Step 2: Be Willing to Change Environments If Needed

Not every structure is capable of holding your next level.
If you've asked, grown, and realigned — and the container stays the same —
it might be time to **walk out of the room you've outgrown.**

That could mean:

- Applying to a new company or role
- Exploring freelance, consulting, or contract work
- Researching spaces that reflect your values, energy, and compensation goals
- Saying no to "good enough" so you can say yes to *deeply aligned*

The version of you that's well-paid, respected, and at peace?
They're not a fantasy.
They're on the other side of this moment.

And this moment is asking you to lead.

Maybe you've been waiting for years —
hoping something would shift.
Hoping someone would notice.
Hoping life would open the door *for* you.

But the truth is…

It's your door to open.
It's your alignment to follow.
It's your life — and it won't rise until *you do*.

Don't delay the decision you already know in your body.
Don't talk yourself out of clarity you've felt a hundred times.

Take the step.
Send the email.
Start the search.
Ask for the raise.
Exit the cycle.
Make the move.

You don't have to leap without wisdom —
but you *do* have to act with integrity.

Because no one is coming to rescue you.
But your future self is already reaching back…
ready to walk you into something better.

4. Becoming the Frequency

Let Your Energy Speak First

The biggest shift doesn't come from what you do.
It comes from **who you are while you do it.**

That's what changes the way people respond to you.
That's what changes the kind of opportunities that find you.
That's what changes the income, the offer, the yes.

It's not hustle.
It's frequency.
It's the quiet radiance of someone who knows: *"I belong in the room."*

You're not trying to get picked.
You're choosing yourself — in posture, in presence, in power.

Ask Yourself This Each Morning:

- How would I show up today if I believed I was already worthy of more?

- How would I speak, walk, work, and lead if I knew abundance was watching?

- How would I treat myself — and my time — if I was already holding the next level?

You don't have to fake confidence.
But you *do* have to start walking like someone who knows they're not behind.

Because you're not.

You're in motion.
You're in rhythm.
You're in alignment with the truth of who you're becoming.

Keep following the Laws.
Keep returning to alignment.
Keep choosing worthiness, clarity, and trust — even when it's quiet.

And when the twelfth Law begins to rise in your life —
you won't have to prove anything anymore.

You'll simply *be* the proof.
And your life… will reflect what you've always been worthy of.

Abundance doesn't just arrive when the numbers change.
It arrives when you become a match for what you've been asking for.

And guess what?

You're already becoming it.

Final Whisper

You Were Always the Channel

You thought money was separate.
Distant.
Something you had to strive for… stretch for… prove yourself worthy of.

But it was never separate.
It was always a mirror.

And now — the reflection has changed.

You've stopped waiting.
You've started walking.
You've returned to the Laws, again and again —
and now, the current has started to move.

Maybe the numbers haven't doubled yet.
Maybe the "big moment" hasn't landed yet.

But you feel it.

The shift.
The frequency.
The readiness.

You've become someone wealth can trust.
Not because you force it — but because you *flow*.

So let the world say what it will.
Let the trends change. Let the markets move.
You are not chasing.
You are not shrinking.
You are not stuck.

You are circulating.
You are anchoring.
You are becoming the channel through which abundance flows.

And now… money moves with you.
Because you move with truth.

This is wealth in motion.
And it begins — with you.

The Path Is Now Yours

You've walked the Laws.
You've remembered your inheritance.
You've faced the patterns that kept you small.
You've taken steps that some never dare to take.

And now?

Now, you know the truth:
You were never waiting for wealth.
Wealth was waiting for *you*.

This is not the end of the journey.
This is the moment you stop searching and start *living* what you've already found.

Let these Laws become your rhythm.
Return to them often.
When you feel stuck — realign.
When you feel rushed — trust the timing.
When you feel lack — remember who you are.

You don't need more strategies.
You don't need more proving.
You don't need more time.

You are not behind.
You are not too late.
You are not too little.
You are not too much.

You are *exactly* who abundance has been waiting to meet.

You are **the evidence** of what devotion makes possible.

You are the **vessel** wealth has been waiting to flow through.

You are the **proof** that peace, purpose, and prosperity do belong together.

So go live this path.
Not louder, but *truer*.
Not faster, but *freer*.
Not for show — but for *real*.

And may your life be the most radiant confirmation that…

Abundance was never hidden from you.
It was hidden *within* you.
And now — it is revealed.

Final Blessing

Wherever you are in this moment…
I want you to know something:

You were never broken.
You were never behind.
And you were never alone in this.

This book may be ending —
but your becoming is just beginning.

The Laws are no longer just ideas you've read.
They are truths you've remembered.
Tools you've embodied.
Pathways you've begun to walk.

Keep going.
Keep returning.
Keep trusting the version of you that led you here.

Because they were right.

You were meant for more.
And now… you are living it.

With all my heart —
may your life overflow with meaning, movement, and miracles.
You are so ready.

With love and light,
From the quiet place that always believed in you.

www.ingramcontent.com/pod-product-compliance
Lightning Source LLC
Chambersburg PA
CBHW062107080426
42734CB00012B/2779